GEORGE O'BRIEN

DANCEHALL DAYS

THE
BLACKSTAFF
PRESS

BELFAST

First published in 1988 by
The Lilliput Press

First published with *The Village of Longing* (as one volume)
in hardback in 1989 by
Viking
Published in paperback in 1990 by
Penguin Books

This Blackstaff Press edition of *Dancehall Days*
is a photolithographic facsimile of the 1990 Penguin edition
printed by Richard Clay Limited, Bungay, Suffolk

This edition of *Dancehall Days* published in 1994 by
The Blackstaff Press Limited
3 Galway Park, Dundonald, Belfast BT16 0AN, Northern Ireland
with the assistance of
The Arts Council of Northern Ireland

Printed in Ireland by ColourBooks Limited

A catalogue record for this book
is available from the British Library

ISBN 0-85640-523-X

for Pam, who should have been there: with love

CONTENTS

You take delight not in a city's seven or seventy wonders,
but in the answer it gives to a question of yours.
Or the question it asks you, forcing you to answer . . .
– Italo Calvino, Invisible Cities

I
CUCKOOS

1

They were tigers. They were liners. They were only slightly less fabulous than jukeboxes, the new 7as and 8s, with their sixty-four seats and automatic transmissions. And though Dublin buses and I went back a long way together, now – I had just been released by the Leaving from boarding-school in Culshiedom – they were more than ever like vessels of desire, Loreleis. Their motors palpitated as though Phil Spector had tuned them. Their familiar ads – so many welcome mats – hymned all I'd pined for: Granby's Sausages, Players Please, Mi-Wadi. The vagaries of their leaps and bounds were surely, I thought, meant to coach me in a risky but fashionable dance, whose moves I – the Chubby Checker of the Sallynoggin run – would soon tame and thrill to. When they breezed along the road beside the bay they turned me into an heroic voyager, alone, aloft, captain and master, drawing smoothly on a Player and practising smoke-rings. I assumed that the fate and soul which I supposedly commanded would present themselves at some pleasant set-down-only stop a few months down the way. How could my present life – nothing but work and family – be the real thing? Like most of my present lives before it, it had to be a missed turn, a detour from the unrocky highway to the city and the city's proper suburbs, pleasure and style, buses' only fitting destination.

For the time being, however, I was not heading into town. I was Monkstown bound. This was where my Da had his new house, his new wife, his new life, his new baby girl. This was where I was supposed to call home (I knew no other word; wished I didn't need one). Eleven d. it cost to get there. That took more than I'd bargained for from the four quid a week I was getting from the International Electronic Company, 3 thanks to my aunt and colleague, Peg. My heroically voyaging sails were in fact a pair of deflated pockets. But I was no more on speaking terms with fact then than I had ever been, so had no bother talking myself out of the high cost of elevenpence. If I couldn't increase cash, I could sustain image, and thus go on pretending that I retained control of something. Drawing on the masochism and self-deception which is mother's milk to hero-voyagers, I puffed myself up with the thought that forking out full fare at least made me a paid-up member of the general public. What I was to those at home and to those I worked with I was afraid to imagine. But the bus took me for an adult. If that cost elevenpence, fair enough. Compared to the free lifts Da gave me – the stuttering Morris Minor; our baleful silences – it was cheap at the price.

And there were the compensations of the route. Lansdowne Road. The Number One Army Band. The country spuriously and therefore happily united through the presence of foreigners. An International! Joe Linnane's crisp tones: 'Kyle to O'Meara, going left . . . . ' Tense faces crowded round the wireless in Lismore. Wasn't O'Meara something to the dentist in Fermoy? Peg used to go: 'Ah, the French were grand,' she reported. But the Welsh – 'Dirty coalminers!' I often wondered how somebody as petite as her – a regular communicant and good to her mother as well – could relish the heaving and rucking. I could only imagine that the city was in her, creator of mysteries and freedoms, of freedoms as mysteries. So when we stood revving for the light to change and I glimpsed the empty stands, I knew Lansdowne Road would do something for me too – that vague, ineffable, impossible, inevitable something which would finally confirm that I'd arrived, that I belonged.

It was only partly on the authority of Peg's experience that I knew the city could remake, enlarge and consolidate me. I had already had some twinges of such a possibility, one or two of them up the way at Lansdowne Road's big first cousin, the RDS. It was fun to see all Ireland on parade there, I supposed. The Nations Cup and the Aga Khan Trophy sounded like the big time. The Number One Army performed prodigious feats of what sounded to me like breaking wind, more impressive for its crispness than its melody; and I craved the true *kitsch* of the Artane Boys in their pink and black, and 'Kelly, the Boy from Killane'. Also disappointing was the unaccountable absence of chair-o-planes and bumpers. It showed poor taste and worse judgments to forego these mechanical analogues of equine callisthenics. But then the horses here were tame creatures, with ankle socks, braided tails, fastidious footwork; mere biological associates of the divot-spraying juggernauts of Lismore point-to-point. All I had to do was look around to see that the mechanical counterparts of these prima donnas were parasols and shooting-sticks, not the vulgar hurdy-gurdy. And Ireland always lost. Why couldn't they, I wondered impatiently, have mounted someone with cavalry in his blood, somebody like Jeff Chandler or Randolph Scott (a shame Grace Kelly was not a man . . .)?

As usual, 'they' were not taking my needs into consideration. Try as they might, however, they did not completely succeed in ignoring me, because as well as showing horses they showed machines. These static brutes were my delight. Horses were for the ancient ways; machines were monuments to the world to come. Horses were the stink and labour of down the country; these machines were of a cleanliness which, together with their power (called horsepower, but I knew it was more mysterious than that), kinned them to godliness. Fired up and roaring, they would anathematize Adam's curse in city accents. I saw myself reflected in the paintwork of their newness. I collected all the glossy brochures I could find, and found myself in them as well. The future was a forklift truck, a Lambretta with panniers. *Some day mine; some day* . . . . The world was Meccano for adults. I was good at Meccano.

I was walking to eternity through Industry Hall.

And when we sprang from the lights at Ailesbury Road, I remembered that here, too, the childish notion that my longing to be something might be satisfied, given time, found more support. This was where Da used to come to get visas for his holidays on the Continent, or to collect something for the Film Society. This was where the flags waved and the pages of my stamp album came alive, and I thought I understood what international meant. It was more than horse-prancing and scrums. It was a realization that we must amount to something if these foreigners came to live here. What that something was remained concealed for the time being amidst the rustle of 5 papers in cool vestibules, the muffled busyness of typewriters and telephones from the rooms beyond. Or rather, the something was that atmospheric *je ne sais quoi*, a combination of the air in those other places where we paid our respects and found perspective, the chapel and the bank. Oh, only let me be the equal of such exquisite establishments!

But after Ailesbury Road I was in no-man's land. By Merrion Gates, even though the houses were once more of a size I felt at home with, the world was dead, a place of names only. The sea was not a sea because it would not roar and crash. All it wanted to do was slap sulkily against the concrete wall, or withdraw to Howth, leaving a black non-beach behind. There was, of course, the giant illuminated Time Ale bottle opposite the Punch Bowl at Booterstown, so for a minute, while the busmen punched the time-clock there, it was possible to imagine that we had not left the city after all. The ad had all the witty effrontery of city style and of downtown's Bovrilorama: beer is larger than life, it said. But this was the last fizzle of bright lights; after it, no life at all was worth talking about until Dun Laoghaire, where at least there was the Top Hat. Blackrock College was a national landmark, no doubt, what with de Valera and things. But I never gave it a second look; I knew all about places like that. Besides, Dev's day was done. The cottages at Williamstown, opposite, were more interesting; they reminded me of the alms-houses in Lismore. And speaking of Lismore, there was a house at the top of the hill before the slope down to Blackrock that would not have been out of place down there, except it had a strange name – Frascati; too unEnglish to fit it properly. I suppose I should have asked Da about it – he was a teacher and would know. But sure it was only an old house. And I was not a tourist. And it was being brought home to me how much safer and simpler things would be if I pretended to be completely indifferent to them.

No *terra* was more *incognita*, though, than Monkstown itself. The bus plunged down the Monkstown Road, and I felt scared. It wasn't the speed, it was the strangeness. The road itself was unnaturally straight. Ailesbury Road was straight, too, but it was supposed to be foreign. There were no flags in Monkstown, so what business did the road have in being different? I eventually concluded that it must have been made by the British for visiting royalty, a miracle in macadam after the rigours of the Irish Sea and the squalid Kingstown water-side, with room to spare for entourage, outriders and loyal beggars cadging a sovereign. Perhaps it was in order to crowd out this last contingent that houses were built along the route. They spoiled the royals' view, but that seemed a small price to pay for such an estimable exercise in civic sanitation, all the more so since the houses were such as to make the regal guest feel that he was among his own. The lower-case 'house' grossly understates how these creations struck me. These were Lodges, Villas, Seats. It was as if all the grandeur and self-possession of the piles I knew in the Blackwater valley were condensed into this one, sheer, untypical stretch of road; into these haughty watering-holes for Wolseys and Rileys whose rooftops were crowned with cubist crucifixes tuned to the latest transmissions from across the water. Only for those aerials and the occasional sough of the mailboat hooter, you'd hardly take this for Ireland at all.

Even the churches in Monkstown were odd. Monkstown Church itself (my stop) was Protestant. I'd never been in a place where that kind of a church was the main landmark. But then I wasn't used to churches that looked like the result of a novena to St Pineapple and Blessed Jelly-mould. Our own drab place was strangely adjacent. It only had a hanky of fore-ground between it and the street, and so seemed oddly unwithdrawn compared to everything else around, imagining itself, apparently, to be in Westland Row or Aungier Street. Yet, like its city brethren, it seemed quite unassuming, as though it had no thought to be taken for anything more than a fairly good-class post-office. It didn't even have a graveyard. But what, only strangeness, could I expect from somewhere which, as I discovered at the top of Carrickbrennan Road, had gone to the trouble of having a castle and had then let it go till it was only a Croke Park for jackdaws; a place which, besides, had never even thought of a river. Ah, Lismore – did I ever offend you!

The reason Monkstown stonework stays with me is that the people do not. And at the time, of all the place's distance and difference from all I'd ever known, the absence of people from the streets was the greatest and most unexpected piece of modernity. It couldn't be right, I thought, surveying the 7 windswept, spotless Monkstown Road: this was the city, there had to be people. They emerged, of course, to go to church and chapel, but these appearances – like those of special guests on variety shows – only drew attention to their general unavailability. Why didn't they stop and gossip, and come over to borrow a saw, and walk up to the match together? Why did they not take to their fine avenues to savour the air of bracing Seapoint and salubrious Salthill? Every so often, the bus would shriek to a halt and an elderly lady in a tweed suit and a miniature greengrocery in her straw hat would struggle aboard with a 'Thank you *so* much' to the conductor, her voice surprisingly firm and carrying, as though formed to address people at a distance. There were hotels in the sidestreets leading to the rocky waterside, which I was glad to see at first, thinking they would bring a bit of life to the place. But they turned out to be encased in a mortifying quiet; dark, lonesome buildings that, being public, had to go by some name, there being no word for the absence of holiday their appearances connoted. Who stayed at them – widows of indigent rectors; bachelor librarians of limited means and fond of a sup; the flotsam of families and the jetsam of marriages; monks of various kinds in the right domicile at last? No trippers. Monkstown, I could see, didn't hold with trippers.

We had neighbours, of course, but I didn't have the remotest notion who they were, what they did, or where they came from. They made no introductions, nor did I. They drove by in their Wartburgs and Simcas; I walked by the wall, cursing their splashes. I cast sheep's eyes at the beautiful Miss Keegan in number 24, and dreamt of taking her to the Top Hat. But it was too far away to ask her to walk home from, and I had never seen her ride a bike (I would have remembered her legs). A taxi was out of the question. They were for turning yourself in at the hospital or, for pleasure, were the birthright of a social class superior to whatever mine was. The dances were dear enough. Not only that, but by the Top Hat ads I saw that it was an awful sophisticated place, and the kind of girls that attended – judging from the photos in 'Going Places with Terry O'Sullivan' in *The Evening Press* – were much too smart for the likes of me, who was, in the world's way, no better than a lapsed boarder, positively sodden behind the ears. What if Miss Keegan was only all amphigory and what she could get out of me? I decided I would cross over when next I saw her coming. 'Nice day,' I'd say; no need not to be adult, after all .... The words stuck in my throat when I did see her. 'Hello,' she said, and passed. Eyes widened, jaw became unhinged. Someone to talk to would have been so nice. But I never did find out her first name.

There should have been tribes of boy and girl Keegans around. The snobby convent and the hardly less classy Brothers at Monkstown Park knew them. They all hadn't left home just because I'd arrived. But they might as well have, because I couldn't lay an eye on them. It never occurred to me that, having lived in Monkstown longer than I, they had probably formed clubs, found activities to share, paired off in dates, held parties and had generally evolved a private social life. I was after the freedom of the streets: they were well beyond that. I thought social life was public: dances, sports, going to the pictures, doing the town. It was unforgivably anti-urban of Monkstown to prove me wrong. I couldn't stand it that the streets were always empty and cars kept whizzing by. Now I was being made to feel private, estranged, unworthy of the dreams which I believed had destined me for Dublin. Longing began an insidious curdle into disenchantment.

When, a little later, I read how Gabriel Conroy lived in Monkstown, I nodded in approval: 'Right again, sir' – that's what it was all right, a world of Gabriels coping with their Gresham nights; or, if anything, a little deader – *unter*-Gabriels waiting for their never-Greshams.

It was a nice new house, nice because new, nice because I had never lived in a new house before. I was used to parlours and pantries and kitchen tables able to seat six. Now I found these were things of the past. A living-room occupied the whole of the ground-floor rear. One corner of it, just, was the kitchen, fenced off by a chest-high wall surmounted by wooden slats reaching to the ceiling. The slats were spaced so that dishes could be passed through them – dead handy. There were barstools under the kitchen counter to sit on while snacking, while waiting for the coffee to perk (they drank mostly coffee) – talk about chic .... The living-room itself was a lake of light and openness, with French windows that gave onto the 9 garden. It was the image of a simple, generous space, like something modern, like America (they'd been on holiday to America). I could easily see why Da and Kay picked it for their new start, instead of something older, more familiar, full of walls which turned space into darkness.

And it was new too because it had machines. Venetian blinds, a fridge, central heating, a garage with a door on a track (no hinges!). There was a yoke like a pocket-sized pneumatic drill for grinding coffee. Da had got himself a new wireless, a Telefunken, compared to which the Sputnik was a tricycle. It seemed the kind of thing Superman would carry in his underpants. Leave it to the Germans . . . . It was reassuring that in one respect, at least, Da identified with the sentiment so frequently repeated by Mr Franz, at work – just as at work I was pleased to hear a foreigner like Mr Franz support what so many Irishmen were saying. The only thing the house lacked was a television set. But I inferred that ownership of such an object would be a violation of Film Society principles, and besides, everything else had been done to be up to the minute; they'd earned the exception. The house even had a phone of its own. And, acme of modernity, there was no bath, just a shower, and the jax was in a separate closet.

The machines and I did not get on, though. Milk from the fridge was a dentist's needle through the bridge of my nose. I didn't know the temperature could be lowered. If it was part of the fridge's job to transfix sinuses, so be it. I felt I was in no position to challenge it. And I was always forgetting to put the shower-curtain inside the shower, so that after a sluice I could have had a swim on the bathroom floor. Since the jax was detached, I had no paper to mop up, so had to use my towel. But then I couldn't dry myself. Shaking only worked for dogs. I discovered the window was placed too awkwardly for me to lean out in the hope that the great Monkstown air would oblige; slapping water from chest and shoulders into the handbasin was also less than satisfactory. And then the inevitable rattle came on the doorknob – 'Will you be long?' – and everything yielded to that combination of cringing and bristling, embarrassment and umbrage, which laces the straitjacket of adolescence.

To prove I wasn't house-broken, there were rules. Some of these struck me as childish, such as always using the back

10

door to get in. Maybe they thought it fun to have a back door, that it was part of the house's newness for them. Or perhaps it was more evidence of privacy, the Monkstown *malaise* of ducking in from the garage. If I were they, I thought, fairly newly-wed, still happy-acting, I would have wanted everyone to see me, and would have loudly availed of the front-door as often as possible. Then I remembered that there never was anyone about.... But, having never yet chanced on a contradiction that I didn't want to lance, I knew there had to be something to this back-door custom: they couldn't be doing it just because it was convenient. Had I a key, there would have been no need to think. Without one, idle speculation became an end in itself. I began attempting the insoluble acrostic of other people's lives. I, *Observer*; they Ximenes. Then there was the shoeless rule. That was one of the explicit ones. It covered the sailcloth which covered the carpet in the hall and on the bottom stair-step. The idea was that the carpet should be made to last, an innocent enough domestic ambition, as I now perceive, but which seemed the height of repression at the time. I was the thing which might not last! To preserve the carpet, no shoes were to be worn indoors. But I had no slippers and felt stupid in my socks. Shoeless I would not go, preferring to stain and scoff my way into bad looks and thunderstorms. Jesus Christ (comforter of carpet) was frequently called upon as aid and witness. What way the head was on me at all, I was often asked? What the *hell* was I thinking about?

I was thinking this is the way the world ends. I was thinking, so this is the life of the dream at last. Life with father. Why the fuck can't you live with lino? We used to. The country was covered with it ... I was witnessing the death of lino. But I had no idea what that meant, apart from there being a connection between new carpet, domestic law and order, a way of life that was tantalizing and forbidding and for which I was unrehearsed, and a sense that all this newness amounted to a mute scream directed at me: *not yours, clear off.* 'Useless article,' 'hopeless case'; the phrases, no matter how often I heard them, hardly began to plumb the black hole of domestic dunderheadedness into which I felt my life had descended. Appalled at my incompetence, bemused by the differences between Monkstown and that future which the past's 11 omissions surely had vouchsafed, I became a numb cuckoo in an ice-bound nest.

If Da shouted, he tried too. He tried to tell me about the holiday in America. But I was wise to that dodge. Earlier he had tried to interest me in the honeymoon, hitch-hiking in France, the ride to the south in the big Citroën with the magic-carpet suspension. Stuff it where the monkey stuffed the nuts, boy! I wasn't at the wedding; I didn't want to be anywhere else. So when he brought up how amusing the TV ads were for Rheingold's (or was it Ballantyne's?) beer – the bottles marching to Sousa, making as if they had legs to kick like cheerleaders – I just thought, bloody hypocrite: TV in Queens was fine, but here he wouldn't give it a second look. He brought home an American summer jacket. 'Feel the weight of it,' he proffered, pleased. I did a fine job of disguising my surprise at its lightness: bloody paper, a small shower would make shit of it. I asked him if he saw any blacks over there (Kennedy was in the White House, the cities were either scabs or ashes). Da explained that the blacks just wanted to be Americans, like everyone else. That'll get them nowhere, said I to myself (a fat lot integration had done for me): they'd be better off burning the whole bloody place down. That's what I wanted to do, only I couldn't find a way· I couldn't even well and truly break a silence.

He had Kay, what did he want with me? He swapped items from the paper with her: he was ignoring me. He'd betrayed the dream. It was all a dreadful mistake, as other family members encouraged me to believe. And everyone knew mistakes could not be rectified or palliated, they could only be detested. But he liked her! Unlike me, he wasn't overawed by her French-inhale smoking style, her swift movements, her knowledge of names mentioned in 'An Irishman's Diary', her mastery of maths. He called her 'hon'. On Sunday mornings they cruised together through the splendid scenery of *The Sunday Times* and *The Observer*, some of it now in colour, even, fags and coffee to hand, the scent of a Sunday lunch growing on them – meatloaf, delightfully spiked with unfamiliar capsicum, and a side of cream-style corn; the pair of them as comfortable as a couple of retired Yanks. After tea, then, the critics on the Third, a crowd of talking newspapers with accents telling how they squirmed and smarted from their own cleverness. Sometimes they got worked up: 'Oh come now – '; 'But surely – '. Why didn't they take their coats off and have at it properly? Then I'd be able to understand them.

Da laughed his flat, dry laugh, sank in his contented armchair, enthralled by vicarious controversy.

'Will you be in this evening?'

Of course I bloody will, what d'you think? If it wasn't a Tech night, where else had I to go? I glowered: 'Yeah.' But I was glad they had a good social life: it was nice being alone in the house, looking after the baby. 'We won't be late. There's a play on the radio, I think.'

'Oh?'

Well, you never know, where's the paper?

As You Fucking Like It! Sure we did that for the Inter. There were only two good bits in it. One was about the cleanliest shift is to kiss, and we all went *smack-smack-smack*. Then another day, when Rosalind said, 'What shall we do with my doublet and hose?' someone in the back in a great take-off of a Dublin accent went, 'Gethem awf ya!' But as for 'Now my co-mates and brothers in exile' and 'All the world's a stage', nothing could be more *passé* to my ears, with the possible exception of the collected works of Dickie Valentine or Guy Mitchell. So I twiddled with the Telefunken's control panel until I was sure the coast was clear, then headed straight for Luxembourg, fingers snapping, tie off, shirt-collar up. I didn't know which was more seductive, 'The Wanderer' or 'Twisting the Night Away' – Dion's sax had the sound of mortal sin in it; Sam Cooke was so light and bouncy and the number's invitation so irresistible . . . . They were both great. And there was no choice necessary: they were all there, all the time. Radio Luxembourg, prototype of heaven, next parish to America.

But even the Station of the Stars – to which I had been faithful since childhood and in whose company I had planned to spend the rest of my life – let me down. Whatever it was about this ostensibly omnipotent receiver, it baulked at 208. At first I thought it was because the evenings were still a bit light (soon, I believed, I would have scientific confirmation of why Lux was stronger after dark: aesthetically, the reason was obvious, rock being the language of darkness – not just of the night, but of the body, too, and the convulsions of its humours). But no, 13 even when the clocks changed and there were fogs that would do justice to 'The Harry Lime Theme', I couldn't get it, though the rest of the Continent came jabbering through in fine style, undaunted by my profane reception.

I tried the short wave. Worse. My eyes narrowed. My jaw clenched. Was it that Luxembourg was perceived in this house as a species of television? I wouldn't be surprised. Did he perhaps unscrew the one valve vital to dancing pleasure? I wouldn't put it past him. Paranoia gripped me like a hobby: the stamps I now collected were, I imagined, meant to douse whatever fire I had. This outlook made home life seem real by lending it the deliberateness of drama, whereas in reality it was all mundane, unthinking casualness. All the head's a stage and all the fuzzy signals and frayed circuits merely pretexts. So that when all was said and done, I still would have my own story, the story which had up until now kept me from a permanent place in Dublin, and which would have a happy ending yet when I at last secured that place. Till then, I could cultivate paranoia for fulfillment.

I broke some rules, too, during those evenings alone with the sleeping child. The front room was never used; that was an implicit rule. So I went in there. This was where the good books were – books in hard Irish; *Franny and Zooey*, *Ship of Fools*; books in French (once upon a time he used to ask me would I like to slit the pages for him. *Would I like . . .* !). There was a record-player too, and I'd have played a record only I was sure I'd break it, so I contented myself by calling the records crap, the work of no names (Leadbelly, Tom Lehrer), apart from *The Best of Sellers*, which I'd heard a bit of on the Light, the – to me – brilliant and brilliantly timely mockery of Céili music.

And there was the portrait. I suppose, looking back on things, that this was why I bothered with that room, that mother-and-child by Brock of Woodstock, Kay and her baby girl. The mother, seated, inclines her head to the white bundle resting in her arms and on her lap. Her face contains great tenderness, rapt, serene absorption. The colours are soft pinks of flesh, sweet greens of new beginnings. Compared to the baby, the mother is very big, a monument, upraised, yet deferential, to the little all-important life it cherishes. I have to force myself to look at it. Then I can't look away. I think it is a a picture of love.

I drift back aimlessly to the living-room. Or, I tip-toe up the carpeted stairs to look on the sleeping child. With luck she'll wake. I'll take her up. She'll blindly clutch my shirt, and I'll feel wanted. She'll whimper from her dream, just like a human. But I'll tell her it's okay; knowing nothing, she doesn't know how well off she is. She settles readily. I look on her with envy.

But back downstairs the bloody old square brass brazier, central to the heat, has gone out on me. Rake, rake; shovel, shovel. Not a spark. The air is filled with ash. Here's the car - 'Fire out again?' He starts in (Kay is checking upstairs): 'I swear to this and that; of all the . . . ' Who does he think he is? *Fucker*. Father!

2

We used to live in Sundrive Road, and there was a 'we' then, or at least it was easier to assume there was since, with a child's pure ego, I believed I was the centre of the family circle, that there would not have been such an entity without me and that all concerned had me to thank for the getting out of ourselves that Dublin provided. The circle may have had a sketchier construction than the later, ostensibly normal, nucleus of Monkstown. But sketchiness wasn't threatening then; it was the stuff of a holiday. If I lived in an improvised family, that seemed an appropriate accompaniment to the lackadaisical, please-yourself ethos of the city. And I was able to relish these arrangements all the more since they so closely resembled the permanent set-up in Lismore (the set-up that was permanent, I thought, for just as long as I wanted it to be, at which point it would be transformed into the eternal bliss of being with Daddy in Sundrive, that road named for my simple, golden dream). Mam accompanied me; Da replaced my Uncle George as my main man; I made an Aunty Chrissy substitute of Peg, who shared the house with Da, even though she worked all week and only had time to play between finishing the clean- 15 ing and starting the Sunday lunch. (Dinner was lunch; I was learning to speak Dublin.) And, adding extra excitement, Granny Royce sometimes came up to see me from Enniscorthy, her soft, indulgent presence both the ultimate confirmation of my being a person of emotional significance and the ultimate reminder of the household's makeshift integrity, as real in its temporariness as a carnival.

For there was nothing only novelty, then. In the mornings I'd wander down for the paper to Keeley's on the Crumlin Road. Waiting to cross, I'd breakfast delightedly on the sweet, unfamiliar fumes of diesel exhaust. The 50s lumbering up from the Barn looked like friendly elephants; the 22s, turning up to Drimnagh, heeled over like great green yachts. Up the way, the Moracrete plant looked so unlike the only other factories I knew – the Cappoquin bacon factory, the tannery in Dungarvan – that it seemed like what they must call monasteries on other planets: it didn't even smell. The Merville milkcarts jogged along with a christmassy jingle, adding to the pleasing music of morning bustle and reminding me again of the classy way the city did things. These carts had tyres on their wheels, not the iron rim that cracked and harshed along the patently insignificant roads of down the country. And I noticed, too, that if the city had to admit that it couldn't do without horses, then it gave them interesting work to do, and often great long drays. Not only did they bring the milk around, they worked for Guinnesses, for CIE, for such fascinating concerns as Tedcastles, McCormack and Heitons (memorialized in bus-ads and in neon signs, rather than for the coal they sold, which merely burned). No tedious ploughing here. No sloppy hauling of those casks of water from the Castle spout. Dublin even had horses drawing those strange little pleasure-hearses that stood by the railings of the Bank of Ireland, run by what I thought must be a large family of brothers, the jarveys. Ah, leave it to Dublin, a multi-horse town and no mistake . . . .

And on Thursday mornings I had an extra treat, the bin men. The palace of varieties that was the daily street became mundane when their act passed by. Their brusque banging and barking put me in mind of circus-men's behaviour. They banged bin lids brazenly, and swaggered on, indifferent to the hissed criticism such rowdiness drew forth (acrobats seemed similarly indifferent to the comments elicited by their bulging crotches). They swung the bins with the lithe ease of athletes and the unerring aim of practised hands. None of them was fat. And they had a fabulous wagon, a semi-cylindrical bin on its bed, compartments with upward-sliding doors containing all the colour and mystery of a Fossett's poster, with (for comic relief, as I saw it) tin baths dangling from hangers at the rear. In Lismore we only had a spavined man called Johnny Gorgeous with a creaky dobbin and a cruddy cart.

But in Lismore we knew Johnny, we knew his little house in Chapel Street, we knew where he took the rubbish. There was no knowing the Dublin bin men. One sure thing, though; they didn't live around our way. I had a feeling that somehow such a state of affairs would not be allowed. Distracted as I might be by their antics, I had still to bear in mind to whose family I belonged and that its city representatives would not dream of living in a locale below their station. My father (BA, HDip) was a schoolteacher with the Christian Brothers, let me not forget it. St Michael's, Inchicore, was not the school Mam would have chosen for her brainy first-born to serve. Its name could only be carved with pride on the palms of the ragamuffins it took in, and it served them right, too, Mam believed. But she knew that John had no stomach for flagellation, and she didn't know how he could stick it otherwise. Thanks be to God, however, we did not live in Ragamuffinland. As though to reassure us, there was the toney Loreto Convent at the corner; 'Oh, a very good school,' I'd heard confabulating wise old heads aver. In case that wasn't enough, weren't we well within a donkey's roar of roads named for the holy places of Ireland – Kildare, Downpatrick, Lismore itself, indeed – which could be invoked as patrons in times of class misgiving, of when what the world was coming to at all needed to be known. But what cared I for nunneries screened by lugubrious evergreens? And as far as patrons were concerned, I gathered from remarks Da passed that this office was being more than adequately discharged by the Behans of Kildare Road.

Sundrive was the real city, monument to the works of man, all the look-alike houses arranged so neatly, people living in a plan. My parents' city. These houses were the future in their time. They were built in the hinterland of history, beyond sites of ambush and executioners' courtyards. These were the 17 houses of peace, of Dublin renewing itself.

What was it like, really? The house was bigger than the labourers' cottages built in ones and twos by the County Council on the outskirts of Lismore but built to the same design. Everything is to the right of the hall and stairs. The hall ends abruptly in a doorless galley of a kitchen, too small to have two people turn at the same time in it. But then it has been made with only one person in mind, and when she's using it she'll have no time for sitting down, will she? So why make space for something for which life's too short? (People living in a plan . . . .) Upstairs, two bedrooms and a box-room. The children, whose arrival can only be prevented by taking absurd psychological and moral risks, can share. (Whoever in the 1940s heard of teenagers? Whoever thought young people might try to translate peace into freedom. They will say nothing and do as they are told, as it is written in these bricks and mortar.) There is a long garden; nobody living here will buy what they can grow. The planners themselves don't, probably. The country isn't moving that quickly. We still retain our roots. If the crop fails, someone will open a chip-shop. There is no place to store a bike, unless it's slung on top of the coal in the outside bunker. It is impossible to put up a garage. A narrow future, a claustrophobic peace. Homage to the safe side.

Except that there is no 'really'. It dissolved in the imagined presence of Seán and Nuala, brave new selves and bridal couches, blushes and giggles: the age-old story and its eternal originality. In the wedding picture his trousers are creased so sharply that they seem capable of cutting the cake and the table it stands on. He is too shy to smile, sobered to a point beyond pleasure by pride in his good fortune: a woman by his side. She, more alive to the moment, smiles candidly, as though replete, an impression confirmed by her high-waisted, tight-fitting dress. Later on, they gaze with pleasure on their sleeping child. Love in Dublin.

They think they'd like another one. But while it ripens, her toxemia festers. It's too far gone. Before she's thirty, Nuala's in her grave, he's a widower, I'm in Lismore. She's just delivered twin cuckoos. Fledgling me is borne to a different nest. Seán is cuckolded by God (the pregnant woman has to cede her life to save her foetus) and by His proxy, nature. The body is

18

betrayed in the body's moment. Love in Dublin. For a long time I'm firmly convinced that he wrapped me up tight, put me in the fine new black-lacquered high-sprung pram they'd bought, got on his bike and pulled me behind him in the pouring rain to Kingsbridge Station. I ask about this, am told it's just a silly dream. But it remains more real to me than anything. I know I'm right. (It's the rain that clinches it.) I know that some day I'll reverse this childish funeral journey. We practise it every summer. One of these summers it'll be perfect.

Aunt Peace lived in Mount Merrion. We had to visit her. We had to visit my mother's Aunt Poll. Now and then, Mam would develop a yen to see someone from Lismore, so we'd go to Inchicore to visit Father Devine, an Oblate, one of Da's contemporaries. The best thing about these visits was the buses. The 46A to Mount Merrion even went by one of the wonders of the modern city, the Donnybrook bus garage, spouse of that more spectacular fifties confidence-builder, the Busaras (at last, I noted with pleasure, buses were getting their due), though Donnybrook had sunk somewhat in my estimation for failing to protect Billy Kelly from the fists of Ray Famechon. Kelly might have been from Derry, but he was definitely one of us – he's Spider's boy, fathered by the nickname into familiarity and fame at once. This lineage was repeated so often before the fight that I mouthed it myself, assertively authoritative, knowing nothing of its history. But it was enjoyable to realize that when I used the phrase I was joining in one of the pastimes of big men: speaking in headlines. Not that the invocation of origins and paternity helped in the event. As Billy – and the whole country – discovered, stunned (as though it had never been known before), a father is no amulet. Still, anyway, though: Fred Tiedt did well in the Olympics. But of course he, I believe, was a busman . . . .
Once beyond the garage we were in Ballyposh. The road got as broad and shady as an avenue. Few buses could be seen, nor could little of anything else: Stillorgan people seemed to have trees on the brain. The place was lousy with foliage. A low hedge ran down the middle of the road. There was a Trees Road. It was amazing to me that here were people who didn't seem interested even in pretending that they were of the city 19

and that the city was of them. They didn't even plant the odd traffic light. Thank God, I thought, for the concrete openness of Crumlin and Kimmage, where there was no doubt about where you were.

Mount Merrion, however, was better, being either above the tree line or having laid down its arboreal arms before the onslaught of new housing. Probably the latter: the ground was very broken all around. In school we had learned in Irish about the fate of Kilcash, and how the felling of trees presaged the fall of houses: *tá deire na coillte ar lár*. But killing and cash had evidently changed in meaning. Now trees were downed that houses be raised. That, I assumed, was history. And in principle I was all for it, ever a fetishist of the new, whether it was a reformed hillock or the latest from Hank Ballard and the Midnighters. When it came to it, though, I didn't much care for Mount Merrion. The houses were fine – semi-detached with white fronts, taken but unused; newlyweds. They had bigger kitchens, rooms to both left and right of hall and stairs, large gardens full of grace and gladioli and maybe a lone bed of lettuce, as though in self-conscious acknowledgment of how the great cabbage-growing tradition, to which we were all born, had become watered down, in inverse relationship to the growth of white-washed cottage into breeze block, Walpamur and mod. cons. But where was their Keeley's, their Moracrete, their big Flood's pub, their Mrs Fox, the Gospel woman (our great gossip)? No 81 snaked handily around the back roads. The air was 'great', no doubt, as the elders all agreed; and having Mount Anville so close by was a godsend, surely. How could anyone be content to live in a mere house, without the scutter of Lambrettas, or the steam and hooters of laundry chimneys, for company? I believed, too, at the time, that Peace and her neighbours thought somewhat along similar lines. That was why they gave their houses nicknames – Manresa, Avoca, St Luke's. We did the same thing at school: it was a way of being informal while acknowledging difference. Peace lived in 'Southwell'. Well, she was from the south . . . . But what did it *mean*? It meant the house had a name.

What were we all doing together at Southwell? Visiting – a very complex synonym for nothing. No doubt my anticlimactic and dismissive reaction to Mount Merrion's combination of exclusivity and banality was (continues to be) reinforced by the same characteristics distinguishing the reception of the Sundrive deputation. The kids were stand-offish, the adults desultory. Those afternoons moved like boats on a bitumen sea. And teatime – looming like the visit's first cause and last resort – could never come quickly enough. We sat out in the famous air, bored. When the boring rain came we sat inside. I was older than my three cousins, and older was better. We had nothing in common. The older girl was quiet, the younger one too small to bother about. Their brother was a Mohawk (sc. ordinary small boy): I can picture him still crashing around, inside and out, roaring the name of his father's trade journal, 'Chemist and Druggist! Chemist and Druggist!' How extraordinarily immature, I said to myself, my nose extending itself obligingly as I looked down it. And him a Dublinman, too. My nearest and queerest. Of course I hated them all. How come they had a Mammy and a Daddy and a new house? They were so well off they didn't have to notice me. Didn't they understand that I was only there to be noticed? – not just at their place, and not just then, but in all the others (there were only others' houses), all the time. After tea, of course, there was no mistaking who was the lucky one. *I* was the one going back to town. *I* was the one who'd see the brilliant Bovril sign rainbow out its letters to the night, probably lighting up the eyes of chemists and druggists.

Yet whenever I did receive attention it was never the kind I wanted. I had high hopes of the Oblates. Granted they were missioners, and they had a grotto at the side of the road by their house and chapel, so they definitely meant business. But it pleased me to believe that their business was not the timber-shivering roar of hell-peddling Redemptorists. Order of Mary Immaculate – ah no, they'd be nice. But in Father Devine's cavernous parlour with its penumbrous paintings and holy smell of beeswax, after the rock cakes *à la* Dunlop were choked down and a temporary lull fell on Mam's exhaustive gospelling of Lismore past and present, I felt the afternoon swivel inexorably in my direction, impelled by our host's large, somewhat protruding, rather liquefactory eyes – the eyes of a 'saintly man'; eyes whose hangdog melancholy could have transfixed and embarrassed me even if their owner's stupid questions hadn't. School, yes; ah, grand, grand; and did I remember my morning and night prayers? Oh, sure, I was a   21 great boy altogether. Da squirmed; but at least he was able to light another fag. Oh, geography was my favourite subject – well, wasn't that a great big word? But speaking of big words, could I tell him this: Constantinople is a very big word, but if you can't spell it you're a big dunce . . . !

'I – t;' and I could puke.

Applause! Acclaim! For unto us is born . . . . All culminating in the detested, the inevitable, intelligence conveyed by some sparrow-fart of 'a little bird', namely that I was not only the hope of the West Waterford intelligentsia but a grand little singer to boot. 'So I hope now that little bird wasn't telling a big fib.'

I baulked, of course; I pouted. I may even have believed that this was one of those battles of wills that I could win (as though I were used to winning them, or something). It wasn't a matter of will, of course, but of infinitely more inflexible manners. Quickly my resistance became 'trying to think', which wasn't easy. It would probably be a sin to do a Johnny Ray or David Whitfield. Walton's advice – 'If you feel like singing, do sing an Irish song' – was all very well, but a solemn delivery of 'Down by the Glenside' struck me as a hymn of the wrong sort (awareness of wrong, its omnipresence and many nuances, was as knee-jerk as genuflecting). So, what *gaisce* would satisfy them (meaning me)? Okay, then: let my vaunted braininess speak for me. I finched out with a finical, unconsciously cynical, sweetness: 'Oró, a bháidín, ag snámh ar an gcuan . . . .'

Yet all my compliance got me nowhere. Going home – after being unctuously (or not in a Lismore accent any more but rather in a quavery contralto) blessed – all the talk was not of me, my conspicuously being good, my musicality. Instead, Mam harped on 'Poor Father Devine, isn't he looking wretched? Oh, he's looking hunted.'

'Ah,' said Da, in his cynical drawl, 'I suppose they had him too long down in Daingean.'

Still, ordeal by infantilizing sentiment and song was considerably less tiresome than being taken seriously, the fate I suffered through Uncle Gregory and his ordeals by sums. He and Aunt Poll lived in Fairview (more great bussing: the 54A from Mount Argus) and, dread it as I might, we absolutely had
22 to visit them, because Poll was one of the four Comerford girls,

Granny Royce's sister, my mother's aunt: therefore she had every right, and considered it her bounden duty, to look on me and see that I was good. Mam thought Poll was perhaps just a little bit touched, because she called Gregory 'ducky', and terms of endearment between spouses were suspect; not 'clean daft' exactly, nor yet the mark of an *óinseach*, but definitely 'simple'. Also Poll was peculiar in being childless. We didn't know too many women like that (and it was always the women who were childless, of course). It was strange to contemplate someone whom nature had entirely overlooked, apparently, and whose soft-hearted manner and roly-poly figure suggested that she had emotion and to spare to lavish but was without a place to put it, which was why she was always gaining weight.

Poll was different, too, because of Gregory. Her three sisters all had married men with whom they had grown up in Enniscorthy, but nothing would do Poll, apparently, only to marry this bald old coot from some hole in Tyrone. At least I assumed Stewartstown was a hole, because that's what I inferred the whole of the North to be, a limbo with purgatorial side-effects, a place behind an iron curtain, poorer even than the God-obliterating Commie countries because it had no Stepinac, no Mindzenty. Sure I could see fine and well what sort those Northerners were. They sent their GNR buses down here, painting them cream and blue, trying to be smart, acting like green wasn't good enough for them . . . . Of course Gregory was on the right side. I mean he was a Nationalist. That, I imagined, was how come he worked now in the General Post Office. Only people with special historical qualifications got jobs there, I assumed, particularly jobs as hard as Gregory's – he had to work all night and couldn't smoke on duty (his palms were dyed mahogany from a lifetime of concealed cigarettes). He must have been in Frongoch or Lincoln with Dev and Seamus Doyle. When he got out it was too risky to go back North, so he convalesced in Enniscorthy, was that it? Or did they meet in Dublin when victory's tide ran full? It was the era of promising proposals. A faith in consummation hung in the air like the scent of cordite, like the scent of sex. They fell in love. They plumped for Fairview because the name described how every prospect seemed then. Or something. I don't know. The past is a frozen mouth, tolerant of whatever   23 words are placed in it, most itself when mute. It reproduces itself in gargoyles known as books.

Perhaps if Gregory had not sprung his sums on me – leaping up from expostulatory converse with a smiling Da on the state of the bloody country, during which he incessantly polished his bony egg-bare head while quite as compulsively feeding Afton-ash to the fireplace – I would have been able for them. If only he could have read them out in a natural voice, instead of in his native torrent of whines and fricatives . . . . Except that he never did sneak up on me: through salad cream and shop cake I could see him coming. And he didn't have to read: the problems were all there on the exam paper, the eleven-plus, through the mindless torture of which some relative of his put children in the North (poor Billy Kelly). 'Thar, nowe,' Gregory would go. 'Take a look at that. Yer Daddy 'n' me have to go out for a wee mingute.' I saw him wink at Da; I felt the women stiffen. 'We won't be long,' pointedly to me.

I bit my pencil till the paint cracked; I would have happily died of lead poisoning. But the exam paper went on sinking its icy, sterile teeth into me, and no relief came nigh. Cruel God! I had to face the fact (again): I was the world's worst at sums. I couldn't have cared less how many men it took to cut an acre given that a square perch was accounted for in three weekends by two urchins and a greyhound (let X equal the number of wet days). Why did sums think that what went on out in the world was a problem? As any fool (or I, at least) could see – especially in Dublin – the world was fine, a sleep-less system of rates and ratios, so blatantly, self-satisfyingly mechanical that the best way to live with it was by mimicking it with machines (beloved buses). Sums had it all wrong: real problems were not compound interest and decimal points. People, alien people, were the problem. Women. Quavery priests. Men who came back and it nearly ten, with grins and inclinations to be gigglesome, but only giving rise to frosty bus-rides downstairs on the 20 back to Dolphin's Barn and sullen bedtime tea.

I was, however, well rewarded for my tours of duty in the unnervingly accessible hinterlands of boredom and embar-rassment. Not that being paid off was part of a plan. There didn't have to be a plan: there was Dublin. The Museum 24 (inseparable from wet days): the Lismore crozier and the fabulous cooperage of the great elk skeleton. Collinstown: Viscounts and Fokker Friendships. We made the pilgrimage to Glasnevin in honour of the major dead. Sundays meant Croke Park: it didn't matter who was playing – though I was glad that so often it was Wexford – because there would be some famous name on show, not to mention the somewhat more exotic, sweaty fruit-women, lugging their unwieldy baskets up and down the terracing: 'Tuppence each th' Willyum payahs!'

The best place was the Zoo. I learned things there. Mandrills came from Africa; llamas from Peru. But nobody could tell me why there were no wild animals from Japan. And it wasn't just an open-air, out-loud geography lesson, me teaching myself in the (usually disappointed) hope that teacher Da would overhear me and approve. The monkeys who pitched their shit at people passing were great gas.

Even when we went somewhere I wasn't interested in, there was some saving grace. The Botanic Gardens I considered a prime bore (apart from the jungle hot-house where at the prompting of one of my favourites, *Martin Rattler*, I sensed delicious danger in the fetid undergrowth and thrilled to see lianas as thick as a child's leg). What pleased me there was the sight of Mam pleased. Green-fingered to a degree herself, her eyes lit up at the riots of colour in their orderly beds. Here, to her eyes, I can now see, was an aesthetic of the Big Houses round Lismore brilliantly at play. But with a difference. Here the cult of property did not supervene. Beauty occupied a zone which seemed at once loftier and more natural, in which the lawns and blooms and foliage were cultivated just for the sake of their own sweet selves. I saw Mam's mouth move in minia-ture *moués*, the way she did when things affected her. Perhaps she was adjusting to the realization that this zone went by the unfamiliar, whispery name of *pleasure*. At any rate, I knew by looking at her that things now would be a little easier for a while. We might even have tea in town.

The enjoyment of inspecting these official city treasures, however, bore no comparison to that of travelling to them. This was the time when buses and I were in the first blush of our romance. Being all pattern and movement, buses defined the city. The predictability of their routes varied with their intriguing oscillations of pace. I loved how they jammed 25 together trying to cross O'Connell Bridge. I loved how they slicked along the South Circular. I loved the busmen. They had strange little battered tin boxes for squatting on. They all wore signet rings – real city stylishness. And speaking of style: what about the way they kept this balance stepping off the backs of open platforms while the bus sped on? Now there was a turn in the human circus performing night and day in the heart of Dublin. I was the only one – except Da maybe – who loved the busmen even when they went on strike for lightweight summer uniforms (which they got): if everybody hated them– '*Too* well off they are,' said Mam, starting the argument – it meant all the more to me that I stay true.

But I never thought of being related to a busman, and there-fore was amazed one evening when, getting off a 22 at Sundrive Road, Granny Royce began to smack the bus's mudguard and go, 'Nick!, Nick!' I knew that neither she nor Mam were very quick around town. They wanted to ride inside all the time with the other women and the shopping bags. They acted as though what was freedom to me was disorientation to them. Still, beating a bus barehanded . . . . But she knew very well what she was doing. The driver slid back his side-window and shouted happily, 'Wisha, how the devil are you, ma'am.' This was Nick White, husband of one of Granny Royce's nieces, Annie, named for Granny. We had a busman in the family, and I never knew it! I often asked about him afterwards, but found nothing out. I never saw him again. He and his wife were never on our visiting list. Was this because they lived in Preston Street? There's no knowing. But there's that smiling face and delighted greeting; chance meeting of an unknown connection; romantic, enigmatic bus-world – kinder to memory than the whole story would be.

We had three ways of getting into town, though generally settled on a 50 or a 22. The 81 didn't get good until Clanbrassil Street, and was good for that street only – was very good then, the Jewish names with -stein and Gold- were wonderfully foreign: yet their butcheries and chandleries were just as dark and cluttered as our own. But both the 50 and 22 got good almost immediately. The 50 snaked around the fringe of the Liberties writhing through impossible narrowness and almost dwarfing the small, tightly-packed houses. But by the Coombe (what did Coombe mean?) – home of Donnelly's, the

26

skinless wonder-sausage, and a strange place called St Nicholas-without-the-Walls – streets widened, as though breadth was the passport to town proper. Unlike the 22, which entered town on a suitably *très chic* note – Cassidy's, Kellett's and Pim's in South Great George's Street – the 50 ran the gauntlet of crumbling, black antiquity: St Patrick's Cathedral, Christchurch Cathedral, great wooden buttresses propagating slums on Cork Hill, the Castle that couldn't be seen. Still, I supposed that some place had to be old; that was what I'd learned in Lismore. Not every bus could be as modern as the 22, and have a synagogue, a Gold Flake factory and the Labour Court in its path. And at least the 50 tried to make a go of it in Dame Street before finally succumbing to the ancient world at its terminus by Trinity.

The main thing was that we were in town. And these were the best days of all, when we had no purpose beyond the ritual of Clerys. Shopping done we'd just spend the afternoon ambling around, taking in the show. I saw Noel Purcell once. Mayor Alfie Byrne accosted us, insisting on a handshake. He spoke in burbles; he patted me on the head. 'Did he want money, Da?' I wondered. 'No, just a vote,' Da said, with a laugh. We ate like royalty at Cafolla's: the ice-cream treats were as colourful as a jukebox's offspring. I heard the cawing of the paper-hawkers: 'Hedl-au-Praiss! He'ldee-Mai-au-Praiss!' Wouldn't it be great to be one of them, or one of their urchin sons, dashing through the buses pausing at termini, shouting? (Wouldn't it be great to be anything – full-time son, even? Oh for the freedom of the typical, of the collective? Oh to be in Dublin . . . .) We had ourselves snapped by one of the numerous street photographers, who deftly peeled a ticket from the wad inside the belt of his gaberdine. Sometimes we went to the dingy counter in Marlborough or Talbot Streets to collect the snaps. They came out grand, unposed and carefree, the city spirit in our mobile postures.

And there was always something new to enjoy in those wonderful nineteen-fifties! If it wasn't the Tóstal it was the Teddy-boys, and if not them, the Unemployed. The teddyers were all style. They were bin-men *en fête*, busmen on a fashion picnic, swaggering and shoulder-conscious, effing from their paths widow-women laden down from a visit to Todd Burns. But the Unemployed were different. They did nothing. They 27 were as fierce as the Mau-Mau. Here they came marching, roaring, the whole street black with them, buses stymied by them, dinner-time disturbed by them. I wasn't able simply to dismiss them as 'a parcel of bums', as Mam did (I felt the room cool, tighten). I dreamt about them. In the dreams the man who was shouting from the top of the Pillar jumped off. He never landed, just kept whistling through surprisingly bright space, a broad smile on his bearded face. I recognized him at once, of course: he was the devil. He was rushing to make work for idle hands, as I understood he had been mandated to do by his first fall. I wake up. It's hard to know what to think. I'm afraid to tell my dreams to anyone; it might mean the end of going downtown.

And, as we all know, nothing happens to us when we're there. We have tea at Robert Roberts or The Log Cabin (Wicklow Street), boiled eggs for the grown-ups, a bit of liver for me to thicken my blood. With luck we'll catch the 5.40 house at the Metropole. I've read that Father John A. V. Burke salutes *The Maggie*. It really is extremely good. Or, for a special treat, we try the Theatre Royal: a film and a show. Maureen Potter blurs by with Jimmy O'Dea in a mangy coat (Biddy Mulligan the Pride of the Coombe in all her moth-eaten glory: an apparition of outrageousness): Harry O'Donovan plays the part of the *amadán*. The sketches are too quick, too topical for me, but I don't care. I'm waiting for Tommy Dando. And here he is in his twice-nightly resurrection from the basement aboard the Phoebus of his electric organ, all pink winks and primrose flashes, a thing of tulle, of organdie trailing clouds of glory in its throbbing, metallic diapason.

The 81 goes *lick-lick-lick* at a fair clip along Clogher Road. I stand near the edge of the open platform to feel brave and let the bus-created breeze course over me deliciously. Here's St Bernadette's: the next stop's ours. I can see the winking-willie flashing at the Sundrive intersection. It's the city's sanctuary lamp. And the only hymn to sing is Tommy Dando's signature tune: 'Keep the Sunny Side Up' (Clap!) 'UP!'

3

But all the big houses in Dublin were wonderful. We usually seemed to end up at the Metropole; it used to have Disney movies like *The Living Desert*, and J. Arthur Rank with his enormous gong was a more or less permanent visitor. I don't remember any cinema having better pictures than the Metropole, but the Carlton had grand banana fritters and you could get a mixed-grill on the mezzanine of at least the Adelphi and the Capitol. The latter, though the least well-sited – shyly, down dead-ended Princes Street, between Metropole and GPO – was undoubtedly the most palatial: patrons went in fear of breaking their necks on the highly shiny terrazzo lobby floor.

The toniest cinema to eat at was the Savoy. That was where I went with Da when he took his French friend, Maurice, out to lunch. A shrivelled figure in a swallow-tailed coat showed us to our table. Numerous others similarly clad attended: who were they – men who'd been asked to leave the priesthood but had been allowed to keep their clerical suits? busmen at the apex of their style's evolutionary potential? Deftly, with indifferent courtesy, they plied us with various *pièces de resistance* – soup of lumber-jacker brown first, then brown-boot stew, and for afters a silver boat of ice-cream with triangular wafer sails, *trés* French. It was definitely not the kind of place where I could not eat all my carrots. And to enforce pleasure, there was a string quartet. Throughout lunch it cut and scraped its way through its Palm Court repertoire, unsmiling policers of brittle feeling, evanescent moods who, once a sitting, cranked themselves up for a climatic 'Wien, du Staat meiner Träume', while the oblivious trenchermen fell to and wallowed in their no less bathetic stew.

The only cinema at which meals were not served, I believe, was the Corinthian, which Da said was called 'the ranch' because of its unvarying menu of horse operas. For most people such fare seemed to be corinthian enough, but not for us. Da's favourite cinema, The Astor, was oddly enough next-door to the ranch – in their proximity a good example to me of the city's anti-uniform, contradictory way of being. The Astor was altogether different – in size, in audience, in attractions: food for thought was all it wanted to provide. Mam and I were 29 never taken there either. (Da had strange taste: he liked the weird American picture that had no fighting – *Marty*.) Neither Mam nor I felt the loss, needless to say. Like everybody else in those days, we were in love with the silver screen, and basically felt grateful for whatever it condescended to depict for us. And it didn't always have to be the early house. We often took our place with all the rest in the huge queues that stretched up and down O'Connell Street, proud and democratic participants in that great trans-Lismore collective, modern life, which had clearly arrived at last, with people jammed in line just like buses.

And what was there not to love? It was the heyday of Alec Guinness and Kenneth More. There was even a sense of patronizing acceptance that the English could hardly be the worst in the world if they could come out with *Doctor in the House* – not to mention *The March Hare*, in which they had Irish actors to make us laugh at ourselves. Ten times better than *The Quiet Man* with its woman pulled along by the hair of the head. Lismore got its moral rag out over that: how dar' them Yanks (that Maureen O'Hara must be a fierce trollop)! And for cinemascope, the screen spread out suggestively.

I looked down on the Palladium, Lismore, from the Metropole queue, and even on its superior competitors, the Desmond, Cappoquin and the Regal, Tallow. None of them had ads *and* shorts *and* maids with trays of ice-cream *in tubs*! In Lismore, Kevi Noonan with the cleft palate tore the tickets and shone the flashlight: no burly, door-wielding officer he. And the films in Dublin never flickered or had woozy soundtracks, much less broke. So there was no need for whoever the owner was to come and castigate the gods, as Doctor Healy did when his features snapped and the lane lads in the fourpennies stamped their feet and chanted, all in rowdy unison, 'We want *Moby Dick*!' Occasionally I sensed a ripple of dissatisfaction in the Dublin audience. 'Cut,' Da explained, when I asked if there was something wrong. They didn't know how lucky they were, I thought, with such small hiccups to put up with. Perhaps queueing up does make them cranky after all.

Pictures were not just for pleasure, however: like everything else, to be any good, they had to rise above the gnawing 30 of the moment's hunger, which, if it remains all we know on earth, must never for an instant be thought of as all we need to know. So, once every couple of years throughout the fifties, a holy picture materialized. Not just things like *The Miracle of Fatima*, in which Our Lady was represented as a streak of pink ectoplasm (a lightly modified fluorescent tube, possibly). Such pictures weren't worth the commotion they created. Doctor Healy discovered this when he moved chairs from his surgery to the Palladium's gangways because we schoolkids had spread word that the nuns – Presentation – enclosed – had received a dispensation from the Bishop to attend. That way we would be sure, we thought, to be let go by our people, permission for a picture on a school night being by no means a certainty. And we could learn from the really good ones: *Never Take No for an Answer*, *Marcellino*, were not about apparitions but about something more miraculous, juvenile protagonists for whom things worked out.

Even Da liked them, particularly *Marcellino*. I was surprised, at first; he never pushed religion. But he did work in a Christian Brothers' school, so I guessed he had been asked to do a bit of overtime. Then I noticed *Film Focus* lying around the house: he must have gone to confession to Father John A. V. Burke, the *Focus* critic. It wasn't until a little time later that I realized that Da spoke well of the two films in question (and never of the *Don Camillo* series, though it pleased large Irish audiences) because movies with kids, movies for kids, were important to him.

I already knew that he thought a lot of films in general. This I discovered when he took me to Youghal for the day the summer *Moby Dick* turned the wharf there into New Bedford (hence the anthem of the Palladium anarchists). 'Go over and touch the windows,' he said – of the new façades. Gingerly, I did. They were all paint – but looked so real! I remember him telling me, disappointedly, afterwards, when he'd seen the finished product, that illusion had not been perfectly sustained after all: in one scene, the sacks on the quay bore the markings of the Irish Sugar Company! He was also slightly put out that day in Youghal because we didn't see Gregory Peck, John Houston or anybody until – I'd been whining, and at last we were on our way to Perks and the bumpers – a car sped by and he cried, like Ahab: 'Look, Seoirs'; Wolf Suschitzky!' – a real-life cameraman, confirmation that there was another 31 world, and that illusionistic windows were also real.

And of course I knew he was in the Film Society.

The Film Society was in North Earl Street above Denson's shoe-shop, just where the 30s set off for Dollymount. As though to prove it was *bona fide* it had its own letterbox, and its name, in Irish as well, Cumann Scannáin na hÉireann, was on a plaque by the entrance. Up then some dusty stairs, and some dustier stairs by the shoe-shop's storeroom, until at last the narrow rise to the third-floor landing, an hallucination of lime-green woodwork, very shiny lino the colour of Savoy soup and unshaded hundred-watt bulbs. There was an office. A lady called Betty ran that. She worked briskly with phone, typewriter and tongue, and she wore black spectacles with winglets on the outside corner of each eyepiece, like those worn by the girls in 'From Nine to Five', an unfunny and unviolent cartoon that the *Independent* ran. Things seemed business-like with Betty around, but lest anyone lose sight of what the Society stood for, there was a still of that wonderful shot of Harry Lime in that Vienna doorway, the playboy of the western conscience himself. And Orson . . . I never heard his name mentioned without the speaker's tone warming to what a Dublin darling that man had been. Orson Welles, bright spark and lavish liver. Disturber of the peace. American dynamo. The youth of a different culture, familiar but fundamentally inaccessible – too quick, too bold. Unnerving combination of birth of a nation and a star is born for Dublin to do anything else but hold him dear in memory, another legend from the limitless past.

Two other rooms opened off the landing, one with projection equipment, speakers and the like; the other, looking out over the street, had a screen and a projector, almost at eye-level with Nelson, and well above bustops – now that was how having arrived felt, though I'm sure I would have felt the same way if the Society met in a Baggot Street basement. It was the people who made it all so sophisticated for me. Those Dublin names – Harper, Toner, Painter, Mulkerns, Waldron, MacLochlainn. The man with the cheroot. The lady who, hail, rain or shine, wore dark glasses. Men sauntering in after short twelve at Marlborough Street, rueing the night before and laughing. Da and me dropping in ('for a minute', he'd say, thinking of Mam and teatime, as if I cared): at the fag-end of a

32

wet afternoon to find – surprisingly, delightfully – that there were others with the same idea, looking for someone to talk to, willing to let the talk ramble and the clock run. 'I see Myles had a good one today, comparing them yokes they have strung across Grafton Street to the lavatory pipework of a big hotel.'

That didn't seem right: 'them yokes' were model atomiums, put up because it was The World's Fair in Brussels. Important. Nuclear. Aluminium. Due to be given to these words' resonances. The new dispensation of the age demanded it. Uranium – pray for us. Thy will be done on earth. World without end. Amen. Who did this Myles think he was? (Who was he?) But I laughed anyway. Everybody else did, and I so badly wanted to be part of it, even then, even for those half-hours that brought us right to the threshold of the rush, so that we'd have to hurry away and call at the Kylemore Bakery for a slab of appeasement before hopping on a 22 for home. Because in the Film Society I saw another Da, a Da without a family, a Da who was a Dublin Seán instead of Lismore John, a Da who, somewhat unexpectedly, had a mind to speak to other grown-ups, who laughed, made others laugh – no longer a silent, chain-smoking withstander of his mother or a man of widower's sorrows. Movies meant life.

But the Film Society was not just sociable, it was social, possessing possibilities of meaning and relevance of which I had neither inkling nor appreciation as a child, when I was too near it, and which I can only recollect now, from too far away, with slack jaw and star-struck eyes. Perhaps the membership did not appreciate what was going on either, since it was disguised as novelty, and since one version of the Irish fifties is that everybody was a child then, polite and more or less perpetually hungry. The novelty was that the Film Society would show movies of quality which otherwise would be denied to Irish audiences – items of such quality that they should not, I learned from Da, be referred to as movies (much less pictures), but as films.

These films were, needless to say, largely foreign. So, the first accomplishment perhaps was to get beyond the ooh-la-la, *La Dolce Vita* barrier, and to invite the audience to take itself seriously by having a look at cinema being intimate, being analytical, being editorial, being (in a word) thoughtful. To do so – inevitably, as far as I can see – meant to make a rude 33 gesture in censorship's direction, since censorship as much as commercial canniness kept Bergman and his mordant men from our shores. And often in North Earl Street I overheard harsh words directed at the censor's office and the official himself was sometimes regarded as not being up to scratch (voices were raised, references made to the Palestine police). This was like cursing a bishop, to my ears, seeing as the censor had his own white little film, with harp and signature, which we had to witness before anything else was screened for us, and what could be more immune to attack than a celluloid seal and office? But here I was in the merry and outspoken company of Da the heretic and his boon companions, who evidently wished for nothing but (like heretics through the ages) to stir a bit of thought, to cause talk, the times being flabby.

Quite possibly, there was a slight missionary aspect to the Film Society, which may have added to its appeal. It was a missionary time, what with the Holy Year, the Marian Year, Father Peyton encircling the country with rosary rallies, the causes of local elect – Edel Quinn, Matt Talbot, Blessed O. Plunkett – forever before us, an atmosphere of expiation so exhaustive that it was impossible to go down town without being threatened by all sorts and conditions of Roman legionaries, armed with flag and rattlebox. If the Film Society were perceived to be against such a social atmosphere, in which nothing was too great to be offered up, to be against something (anything), to be – God save the mark! – in favour of pleasure and the instruction it provides, not to mention *vice versa*, then that helped it thrive. It's preferable, however, to believe that what attracted much of the membership was the presumption of privacy, responsibility and similar anti-corporatist virtues which paying a membership fee secured, identification with which the films being screened ratified. As for the uncountable numbers who may have joined to peer down the cleavage of Anna Magnani or Anita Ekberg, such tit as there was came submerged in subtitles – so they didn't count.

At any rate, and for whatever reason, thrive the Society did. It found a public, and whatever the public found in it, more joined year after year. The season, as the series of screenings was called, was forced to move from the baby Astor to the
34 latest thing in cinema-going at the time, the State Theatre,

Phibsboro, a thousand-seater with an exotic sound system. People had to be turned away. Then down the country wanted to join in. Da went to Mullingar, to Limerick, even back to Enniscorthy (lair of patriots), to help found branches, though these often withered, to be replaced it seems by the silence out of which they had initially clamoured, and for whose existence Dublin was no doubt blamed, as so often.

They sat, the company of a thousand, including my knowledgeable Daddy and the unforgettable woman who, I heard, cried all the way through *The Seventh Seal*, without leaving and without ceasing, and saw for the most part what they already knew but what perhaps their rivals – the Pioneers, say, or the Legion of Mary – had made it difficult for them to realize. Which of them had never seen an Umberto D? And which of them had not felt moved in their familiar lives by the strange, yet recognizable, sight of him – there, at a distance, in perspective, mobile after a fashion yet touchingly lacking in elusiveness, unlike his counterpart shuffling along Dorset Street. If there was a *Bicycle Thieves* there had to be an Unemployed. But wasn't it a cheek of those Italians to make a whole opera and tragedy out of a push-bike? But wasn't it the truth, as well – as plain as day? And can that be Italy, neither religious nor fascist nor a nursery for tenors? There's Rome, its eternal aspect now, unnervingly, the poor – who, as our unclerical birthright shows us every day, are always with us.

This audience begins to imagine. It forsakes for a while the kiss at sunset and Max Steiner's swelling strings. Instead it forms a temporary tolerance for the black and white of dusty streets, for the ways of ordinariness and the modest yet urgent hope of surviving their humiliations. It sees that life in the mean streets only appears to be a matter of black and white. Perhaps here, over the course of an hour, sympathy is released from latency. Perhaps there's the surprise of discovering how much of life is seen through the puce-coloured spectacles of class. This audience rubs a window. It raises, for the time being, a temporary shelter against the miserable drizzle of injunctions and exhortations to black-and-whiteness, straight-and-narrowness, that befogs the brightest day. Behind their backs, the machine dreams on, its intense eye piercing dim, fog-filled confines. This audience has something to look up to.

35

Was it to live the different movies made that Da went to France? He went to Rocamadour to stay with Maurice, a place no less miraculous than Lourdes, not because of what had happened there, of what might happen, but because it had implausibly clung for centuries to its cliff, as though nothing could be more natural than to carve a domicile out of stone. The people ate frogs' legs and snails — they found a way of eating them. They may have been (they must have been) starving; still they were stubborn enough to put a bold face on things. When all fruits fail . . . . No cuisine without famine. No cliffs without dwellings. No style without chaos.

Da heard it all in Piaf's candid, brazen larynx. *Je ne regrette rien*. He saw it in *La Grande Illusion*, where each frame is so full it looks like a cross-section, the screen itself a cell which shows constraint and implies liberty. He saw that escape can be unexpectedly rewarded with love in the mountains, and that escape is sponsored by spontaneity, and that love is the precondition of freedom. He may have relished the film's redefinition of Robert Gregory and Kiltartan Man. He may even have seen that an illusion is only as great as the human need creating it. Perhaps (since he remains the doubt I give myself the benefit of) . . .

We went in the Henry Street entrance, in itself a surprise because I never thought the GPO would have such a private-feeling doorway. It was somewhat dark. There was an air of men smoking and moving purposefully, but that may only be how I had imagined Radio Éireann would be before we got there (memory and imagination: what is the world compared to them?). There was a lift, of course, also a liftman. All the most important places had them. There was a lift and a liftman in a pillbox kind of hat in Brown Thomas's. And were we two not important people? Nothing but a smooth machine for us today. My Daddy was going to give a talk on the wireless.

Upstairs there was a lobby, with a radio in it the size of a coffin, and a man sat in a swimming pool of an armchair listening to it. Perhaps he was the man who played 'O'Donnell Abu' on the harp before the programmes proper started, just to give everyone a minute to get ready and get us in the proper holyish mood – except it was only women who ever played the harp, wasn't it? Whoever he was, he stupidly paid us no attention. But in a minute that didn't matter, as we were summoned by a beckoning man in shirt sleeves who approached from the broad hallway off the lobby. His name was Eddie, as I found out on our way down the hall with him: people were calling him, stopping him. I was impressed that somebody not wearing a suit could be so much in demand.

I was told to stay where I was and Da was led into a room. Down the way a bit, however, I saw what I took for a window – at least I would be able to watch the buses while the grown-ups went about their secret business. But it wasn't a window at all; it was a glass wall and there was Da looking at Eddie who was behind a similar glass wall. Da was mouthing soundlessly from a paper. Eddie raised a finger to him. There was an explosion of jabberwocky playback. Then soundlessness again. Wheels of tape. Clean, artificially lit world of brain work.

I assumed all that remained was for us to return in triumph to Sundrive, turn the knob, and there, larger than life because present in an attenuated form – as though he were finally giving expression to our relationship (and, to make the moment sweeter, didn't know it) – he'd be. But we had to wait. Of course: I was dealing with grown-ups. Not too long, however: this was great Dublin, after all, where things happen – so it would surely happen. And surely happen it did: a week or two later we all – Mam, Peg, Da, me: my picture of the happy family – crowded around the Bush.

The familiar theme came through, something brassy, kinetic, I seem to remember (by Prokofiev?). 'Film Magazine,' said the voice, 'introduced by Maxwell Sweeney', who then spoke.

'Eddie,' I shouted: *I know him.* And then I thought, 'But – Janey, just like a film star: I didn't know the wireless made you that famous.' Maybe Da . . . ?

It was a strange programme – no music, just different voices looped together by clever Eddie MacS. At length Da began. He was brilliant: two solid minutes' worth about a shorts festival somewhere in the Pyrenees. It was news, it was travel, it was nicer weather, it was words in French, it was better than Bing Crosby singing 'Around the World'.

When it was over I waited for something to happen. Nothing did. (Well, Peg put the kettle on.) There was silence. 37

It felt cold, the same as it did the night Chrissy sang in the St Patrick's Night concert and I wasn't allowed to hear her. But didn't they understand? He was great. We should be going out for ice-cream. I took to whining, as usual, and as usual was sent sulking off to bed. The pink evening expired slowly beyond Clondalkin, as usual. So nothing had changed – maybe he wasn't all that great: maybe it took being on the BBC to make a difference . . .

All I'd wanted or expected was a wallow in his radio fame, but there was more: first, the Confirmation show, then 'Boy Wanted' – starring *me*! Da became a leading light in the Junior Film Society. Going to a picture was all very well, it seemed, but how about trying to make one? He found a way of being a teacher in his hobby-time, a way of making more of himself, or perhaps attempting to turn to material and active account some of what he may have seen in Truffaut and De Sica, that there was no project too humble, that there was no such thing as the culturally insignificant, that there was now available a collective recording machine – the movie camera – which could enlarge and mobilize and change forever our posed, box-camera images of ourselves, the medium shot in Sunday suit which expressed an ethos and obscured its context.

And, as I now appreciate, this commitment had to be the result of a decision, because it entailed the use of materials, money and resources, some of which were the Society's property. Da didn't have automatic access to any of it, I assume, because no Society would survive without controls, so he had to make a case for what he wanted to do, and be prepared to wrangle – not because everyone resisted him but because institutions of whatever kind seem to create wrangles (think of families). And even if all went smoothly, I must supply some tension, some drama, to remind myself of his unusual commitment, which seems, looking back on it, to be akin to desire in its normality (I hear him still speaking quietly, proudly, of staying up late helping to edit *Mise Éire*).

Of course Confirmation was going to be a big deal even without the film. For once, the Church seemed willing to cherish, rather than chastize, us. It was the last of the sacraments for a while. It meant the inauguration of long trousers and the first wrist-watch and, to make sure we knew what

38

such symbols connoted, we had the Pledge administered to us – no drink till we were twenty-one, which caused confusion in Swiss Cottage: was it proper to have the sherry in the trifle, the great day's obligatory dessert, the secular viaticum for the journey to manhood, now officially begun? The Bishop would be in town, and all the clergy for miles around would turn themselves into his altar boys for the occasion. We had to take an extra name, to signify no doubt the extra dimension of identity that was being conferred on us. Almost to a maneen, we selected Joseph. Worker, donkey-driver, related to the godhead by a happy accident of birth: he was avatar and patron: one of ourselves.

All was exciting enough – so when Da stepped from the twenty-past three on that Whit Saturday with the odd-looking container slung over his shoulder it all seemed part of the novel event, even though I had no idea what was in it. But a ciné-camera – to make a picture! Talk about 'Veni, Creator'! I thought, oh leave it to him to add the city touch to the proceedings and make me marvellously different. And there he was the following morning, tracking us as we marched up Fernville, crouching by Parks Road to make a happy ambush on the girls parading demurely from the Presentation. Even more astonishingly there he was during Confirmation itself, over in the men's aisle with one foot braced on the seat and the other against the armrest, looking for all the world like the heroic standard-bearing icon of labour and of progress, who strains forever upward and forward on revolutionary posters.

How did he do it? He must have passed himself off as someone from the Catholic Truth Society, an agent of Verismo House; *plámásed* his way past canon and curate as a member of the Irish Chrism Society, man-and-boy believer in a Godly Cinema for a Saintly People. That's what I like to imagine. But I remind myself that he didn't start shooting inside until the proceedings were well under way and that he didn't shoot more than five minutes' worth. So he probably just went in and did it without anyone's permission; he had already packed up and gone by the time the celebrants realized that what they had just heard was the whirring of a camera, not the flutterings of the knowledge-bearing dove. Guerrilla cinema. That's the style! (Wasn't one of the reasons I loved him because he was a guerrilla parent?)

But, as I saw later on that summer at the premiere, the production was more provocative than the product. There was a nice shot of Pat Lyons as we boys waddled along (the dressage of Christ's Fianna), our faces and rosettes a grainy pallor against the grey of everything else. Mary Fleming had a beautiful bright smile, brighter than her dress's pure white. I don't think I'd ever seen it properly before. But for the daring raid on the chapel, religion got its revenge: it was all spectrally white with few discernible features, from unexpected sunshine flooding through the windows over the apse. And not alone that, but where was I? He seemed to have forgotten my central status, without which the whole effort seemed a complete anticlimax. Minus me, all ordinariness a gross fabrication.

My hour arrived, however (why did I doubt him?), with 'Boy Wanted'. Unlike Confirmation, which now I could forgive – a test-run to make sure he could use the thing, thus unworthy of me – 'Boy Wanted' (eight minutes) was an original. It had a story and everything (meaning me). The Phoenix Park, morning. A (borrowed) Morris Minor, one of its side windows open a chink, a camera on the passenger seat inside. A thief – yours truly – happens by, knacky-fingered, fleet of foot. Spies window of opportunity, acts, is hailed in hamfisted hieroglyphics by large member of Junior Film Society. Flees. Film Society fatty proves fleeter. Rugby tackle fells filcher. The End.

I leaned against the side of the Morris Minor, disgusted, the bitter sweetness of finding myself at the margins of his admirable efforts coursing through me. I represented the very passivity which the project was helping everybody else in it to overcome. Why did I feel like somebody's plaything? Why did Da have to spend so much time with the other lads, explaining? I should be part of that group. *Ich bin ein Dubliner!* I hated it that the teacher-pupil relationship seemed more substantial than the father-son one, being able to draw on familiarity, continuity, a group's shared goal. What I thought would be a collaboration between us turned out to be a collision.

It wasn't 'Boy Wanted' I'd call this, I said sullenly to myself, looking at the insipid, wooden allegation of me on the screen. It's – it's – But my dream (also entitled 'boy wanted') wouldn't let me. Fuck film! It was too real: it was not real enough.

4

This is what the voices said. They said:

'Only for the blasted Film Society, it would never have happened.'

'Ah, it was all that out half-the-night with that oul' *Mise Éire* business.

'She married him, anyhow. She saw her best chance – and of course John was always too soft. Wouldn't say boo to a goose.'

'Bloody fool – and she half his age: well, I wouldn't like her job trying to teach that old dog new tricks.'

'Hitch-hiking, that's what she has him at – at his age: did you ever hear the like? That's how they spent the honeymoon. I suppose that's more what she learned in America. She was in America, y'know, tried to push in there, but the Yanks weren't having her – they were too fly for her. But sure here . . . . '

'Men are such awful eejits!'

'And of course Sundrive Road wasn't good enough for her. Nothing would do her but Monkstown. And she from Prussia Street. The cheek of her. Nothing but a social climber – going in there among them educated boys; a know-nothing. A jumped-up nothing! An able dealer' (a rhyme in Lismore's eighteenth-century accent).

'They go off to Donegal and places, climbing. And staying in the hostels, what d'you call the thing? *An Óige*, that's it. *An Óige* how are you?! At this hour of his life; isn't he a desperate foolah?'

'And where's this Prussia Street is?'

'In the heart of the cattle-market – and hasn't she the look of it! On the way to the Zoo, there; where them pens are.'

'Oh my God!'

'Imagine waking up to that racket every morning!'

'Sure Sundrive Road was too good for her.'

'Of course it was.'

'And did you see the oul' mother – the fallen arches of her, the dropped stomach.'

And so it came about that in these Monkstown years there was a death in the family. The victim was the institution itself, the O'Brien family, its authority and integrity. The royal we turned into Humpty-Dumpty. Not the new family in Monkstown. It went its own way regardless, persisting in the   41 freedom and independence which originally animated it and which created such animus in others. That family increased, and if my very slender acquaintance with it is anything to go by, all concerned seemed fulfilled, secure, until eventually, though all too soon, death – the death that is not metaphor, I mean – had its way there as well. But in my time – before I brokenheartedly discovered that I would have to live my own life after all – what I saw happening, though I could hardly take it in, was the self-willed yet seemingly involuntary eclipse of the old Lismore hegemony·

The chorus elicited by Monkstown was all the more intense and unremitting because it was the swansong of a process begun years before, at the beginning of my boarding-school sojourn, when Chrissy got married and Georgie disappeared. These two events did not occur all that closely together. In my memory, though, they are welded as one: a joint presence with the immensity and force of a wrecking ball, with something too of the desolation and deliberate irreparability which that machine leaves in its wake. Not that the events were bad in themselves, and even if they had been they would not be the first to earn a stern reaction. Ours was a family like any other, after all, with rifts and banishments the order of the day. People were out with each other, then just as suddenly were not: it was all as intense and wasteful as the whirligig of fortune in a minor duchy. The difference in the case of Chris and Geo was the finality. They were consigned to moral Coventry, left severely alone, as unredeemable as sinners from the flames of hell, collaborators with an enemy identified as their own selves.

Chrissy spent her early married life in a flat above a shop in Main Street (oh how she had fallen: she didn't even have a house!). She wheeled her first-born up and down the town one summer long. I saw her every day. The lads that I hung out with all saw her, all said hello. I never did. I was told that whatever I did, I shouldn't speak. Not long after, the moral Coventry turned into a physical one: Chrissy moved to another town. I carried on at boarding school, missing her parcels of HP Sauce and cherry cake, her five-bob postal orders. By trying not to think of her, by trying not to picture her new life, her babies, I reproduced the silence that presaged her exile. That silence, Mam assured me, was for my own good, the same as everything else I hated or misunderstood, from tapioca to my mother's death. My school silence arose from having nobody to tell. I felt a loved one had been obliterated. I felt deprived of number two Mammy. There never had been a seriousness like this, as far as I could remember. I couldn't talk. I didn't know how to mourn. In the darkness from which tears might have arisen, memories took root, monstrous, slow-maturing fungi, soul food, soul hunger.

Even more mysteriously, Georgie went away. I came home from school on holiday and when he didn't show at suppertime asked idly where he was. 'Gone,' tolled the reply. Mam wasn't sure where: she thought probably to Chrissy in Cahir. A long time afterwards we heard he was in England, married. No attempt was ever made, as far as I know, to pursue him. When he came back it was in his own time, and only for a holiday, and long after it was possible to reopen the shed in which he and his father had hammered things out, in which he had tried against unarticulated odds – as all must – to give his own life a shape, finding at last that it was only possible to do so in another country, a country he had turned his back on many years before, returning to Lismore in hopes of realizing himself there . . . . So lives go through their unforeseeable, appointed rounds, lured ineluctably through the ordeal of love in exile via the ordeal of lovelessness at home.

No doubt there was much more going on then than I was aware of, more perhaps than even the participants themselves could handle properly. Who can say what's buried in the lives of people? – not the people themselves. They simply reach an awful point at which nothing more can be said. Then action blunders in, singular and irretrievable. Yet in its wake a deeper silence wells for which a gloss must needs be found if all is not to be lost, if all lives are not to be spoken of as the unexceptional mean of rage and need, if the only version of seriousness is not to be extremism, the quelled world of silence that follows explosions.

I didn't know exactly what a dropped stomach was, but I knew from the tone that it was first cousin to knocked knees, pigeon chests, fluke eyes, mallet skulls, elephant arses and all the rest. If people were belittled by their bodies, let them be mocked and denied seriousness: that was standard practice for just about everyone I was reared with. Looking down on

43

Prussia Street was also second nature, and again as much on the grounds of aesthetic connotations as of class. It was necessary to come from a place that looked right in order to be right, and Kay's bailiwick had neither a pleasing image (cattle in pens being a species of brutal materialism which cattle in fields naively disguise) nor a pleasant sound. Sound was important too. There seemed to be a diktat: never marry a girl from Ringaskiddy, keep clear of bank-clerks from Mullinahone. It was as if there could be no sense of value without a sense of sin and devilishness, no self beyond one that an enemy evinced (oh my colonized people!) . . . Prussia was foreign and ugly, a dream of enmity, pompous homeland of gutteral brass-bands and unconscionable steel which scythed down the flower of a generation (Mam's), enemy of the clever French and Dev's own strict Spaniards, old friends of Ireland, whom Da was content to visit when his head was on the right way, in the good old days, when he could still be thought a creature of circumstance – a little better off than some, no doubt, with a profession and a Dublin posting, but essentially crushed and mournful and one of ourselves . . . . Imaginations worked overtime looking for combinations in its limited index of associations and received images so that ranks could be firmly closed against the Prussian revolution, the marriage to Dublin and the totally unexpected family, Da. Every so often out of the 'phone came a barrage of resentment and frustration, blaming Kay for an image which she had not fabricated, denouncing Da for killing Sundrive. And even these thoughts, if that's what they were, would have been comprehensible if their creators had been able to acknowledge them as simply a set of possibilities, an interpretation, an attestation of strangeness knowing itself subject to the corrective of mind-opening experience. But the aim was not to deal in forms of words and hermeneutical niceties – the aim was to use weapons. And no doubt, that death hit everybody. Isolated Monkstown spawned unfamilial satellites of isolation. Now Peg saw that she and Da would not be growing old together, silently: her years of anonymity were about to receive public acknowledgement beside some bell on the front door of an apartment house (itself an aborted home) in Dartmouth Road and Garville Avenue. There, complaining of the noise made by the three typists sharing upstairs, she would discover how long ago her dancehall days had ended and turn up the volume of her TV. Now Mam would never come to live in Dublin. Old age stretched out before her in Lismore; neighbours in to see she'd eaten, to check the fire. Now, for the first time in forty years or more, she was alone and childless, the rosary beads her lifeline. And I, the common non-functioning link between them all – what now was I, or who?

Wrong, wrong, wrong. Prussia Street was very interesting. All kinds of buses made for it from the quays heading for the unknown reaches of the far north-west side, Blanchardstown of the hospital, the Navan Road. And when I visited Kay's house, I was pleasantly surprised to find it had Swiss Cottage size, damp age and huge dark furniture. It was not a hovel lapped in cowshit, and the satirical representations of its locale's variation on *rus in urbis* so confidently projected were off the mark. Since this was where Kay and her family were from, there was an easy traffic of people in and out, talk of one son overseas, and of another living on Botanic Avenue. Kay's mother was a heavy warm-hearted woman, slow, but not slow dull, slow watchful, tender, fond of putting on the kettle and of whipping up a bite. People lived there. It all struck me as disarmingly normal. Suddenly, there was nothing to think, and I didn't know what to think.

One evening, even, the household showed itself to be capable of getting above itself, of consolidating its normality by demonstrating that it wasn't enslaved to it. Kay and Da and I dropped by late – from the Film Society, no doubt – to find the front room ringing with laughter and the chime of bottle and glass. (It was, I think, the first time I'd seen drink in a house where there was not a funeral.) Everyone seemed in right form, and before long (or at any rate it didn't seem long), Da was wearing a Gregoryoid Fairview grin. The friends and neighbours standing around looked great, definitions of male careers of a certain grade and shapelessness such as are connoted by the common nouns jobber and coper, handler and runner, and by such articles of dress as ties doing the job of belts, wellingtons with the tops folded over, *cáibíns* worn back to front and similar insults to the felt millinery fraternity, the whole disarray transfigured by cast-off or mislaid gentle- 45 man's waistcoat of canary yellow. None of those present was dressed like this, needless to say: that evening they presented themselves as victims of their families' Christmas duty, each one a lino showroom of Argyle, checks, and Fairisle – but there was a certain splayed look to their features and a list to their demeanour to suggest lack of rigidity in other spheres.

When sufficient drink had been taken, voices were raised requesting turns (Father Devine, be thou my guide!), but – what a grand crowd – nobody minded when I demurred. They sang themselves and one little man soberly recited, with a swaying motion, 'The Wesleyan Chapel', about the couple who had bought a new house and wanted to know where the nearest W.C. was; so they wrote off, and received by return an elaborate prospectus for a W.C. with plush kneelers, hours of opening, sermons, baptisms and everything else necessary to salvation. The room began to reel with laughter. We became the people Brendan Behan knew, naughty and natural and knowing no harm. And to follow, Da and Kay sang a duet: 'Rickety Tickety Tin' – a fake folk-song, about blood and murder and morality's victory: the perpetrator confesses all, because 'lying she knew was a sin'. Silly, silly adults – I shrieked with laughter, slightly lightheaded, as though undreamt of weights had been lifted off my mind.

But this was not where Kay lived, not really. She had a room in her grandmother's house on the other side of the North Circular. But how could that be, I wondered. Her parents let her do this? She wished to be a cuckoo by design? She loved her grandmother, that was all. I was surprised again. There was nothing terminal about it, there was no rift – it may have even been a generous act: all concerned seemed still the best of friends! On top of which, Kay was smart. From all I'd heard she couldn't have had much schooling. There were no fine Loretos at the bottom of her road. And who belonging to her received degrees, taught school or otherwise attained the petit-bourgeois heaven of work sans dirt? But there she was, nevertheless, a genius at unendearing sums, a confidante of high-ups in insurance companies. The Monkstown living-room table became snowed under with actuarial spread-sheets. The grass-hopperish sound of the manual adding-machine chattered late into the night. What was I supposed to make of that? Enmity spoke a language which failed to describe accurately the world as I found it. The trouble was it spoke a language more complex and authoritative than any that world cared to speak.

The trouble was the present had a language but no words. The 'phone rang, creating a major verb. I baby-sat and generated unutterable speeches. For common nouns we had tears, flights up the stairs, doors banging, Da solemnly, ploddingly, following. So I never got to know Kay, or she me.

I squirmed to see an adult cry. I knew what tears meant: I was a gifted sprinkler as a child. Boarding-school eventually turned me off at the mains, though: surviving it meant swearing nothing ever again would make me shed a tear. Now I wanted to cry, but had no audience in Monkstown. The audience I had was the people Monkstown knew only as the enemy. But when I cried to them it merely caused the 'phone to ring. The more it rang, the greater chill I felt. Soon nobody was talking. I learned that silence, too, could be violent.

Lismore had been the first exile, inevitable but temporary. The second banishing was boarding-school, also temporary, but far less justifiable. And now, when everything seemed set, when there was no place else to send me, when finally it seemed I was on the point of becoming like everybody else – with even a mother (or at least a Chrissy substitute), and not just mother but Dubliner as well, someone at last who knew all I wanted to know about the city of my dreams, the city and my dreams – I only felt unwanted. So what was I, or who?

I was a sore thumb. I was a ghost. I was a wedding gift from ancient history. I was the homage resentment pays to impotence, an imageless irritant, a spy in the house of love.

The telephone. It's a symbol (of course . . .). Colloquy with a dark receiver. Exchange and throughput. Dialling facelessness. The film violence of cutting someone off, of being cut off. The weapon of choice for the genteel ambush. The bridging of distance which only draws attention to distance. How important language becomes without the body it's embedded in. The telephone: mortal enemy of the cup of tea . . .

That's way of talking about that small guerrilla action, those many years ago.

Another way – the voices come lapping in, their passion and rectitude shrivelling the intervening, silent decades – would 47 be to try·to discover what those voices really meant (that slippery 'really'!).

I hear them damning Da for the sin of change. He should have stayed neutered in widowerhood (what release did he have in that body-hating culture?): he should have stayed choiceless and loveless. He had no right to start over. How dare he believe in the romance of the second chance? Look at the cut of him, upholding desire, even optimism (no wonder they thought he'd end up in America). Sure who in his right mind . . . . Didn't everybody know that marriage was either for the young and foolish – the mot tired of baking Jacob's biscuits gives herself to the plumber's apprentice; brawny wardsmaid from the Mater overwhelms bespectacled insurance clerk. Or else it was for newly orphaned middle-aged countrymen: John Joe, the acres secure at last – praise be to Death the provider – approaches in stealth and hobnailed boots the canon's housekeeper. But here, now – lo and behold! – an act of generational and cultural miscegenation in our very own midst . . .

Da and Kay had sinned against pattern. They had committed change, and had (oh horrid hubris) assumed that they were free to do so. They had caused thought. Proud things – they won't have luck! And as to her alternative destiny, considered her unentitled to the franchise of partnership, home, happiness, sex and everything else due a desire for a full life. Perhaps she seemed insufficiently self-sacrificial. Perhaps she (being in love) tactlessly neglected to sue for their *nihil obstat*. Was she so shamelessly imbued with the Dublin looseness of Prussia Street that she was sufficiently freeborn never to consider the very existence of psychic property rights? Whatever hopes of fulfillment Kay may have realized in Monkstown, in marriage, were considered to be as spurious as a successful Sweep ticket, a revelation of how life's distressing unpredictability expresses itself in dumb luck and blind fortune, gods that only pagans worship, the same base, humanoid gods that made city life a lottery and a holy show. Speaking from lofty judgment seats – apparently in some unearthly location beyond frailty, beyond desire – did these voices finally mean to say that all they could acknowledge was a marriage between opportunism and self-deception? I don't know.

Hovering between language and silence, all I can do now is what I did then: speculate, analyze, imagine. The only life I had was an inner life. I lived off it anorectically, demanding that my resources alone could reduce my world of words and non-words to comprehensibility. The wasting cure, the hunger strike more deadly than the cause creating it. But it was all too serious to live with, too unexpectedly serious, and not at all my version of love in Dublin.

5

It was March, the sixth month of our winter; a Sunday.

'Seoirse!' Da's voice boomed up the stairs.

I don't know why I was in my room. Perhaps the storm had been already rumbling, or I knew one was going to break, having become so sensitive to atmospheric pressure.

I remember coming to the head of the stairs. I remember roaring, 'Get out! GET OUT!'

I remember walking back into the room, reaching under the bed for the suitcase – the case that used to be his, that used to bring the Christmas gifts – and beginning to pack. I had as much feeling in me as that old leather-and-metal portmanteau, as the mound of dirty shirts and underpants which I'd built up, like an image of a depression, in the cupboard of the night stand. I felt as much alive as a sheet of blotting-paper, a palimpsest in others' hands.

Then, steps on the stairs, and Kay bustled in: 'Don't. Put the bag away. He didn't mean it.' Her face was flushed.

So just as dully I put the clothes back in their festering hide, swung away the bag, and I can remember seeing grey, then, and smoke rising from the smaller, closer-together houses up the road, so I suppose I must have gone out, walked up Mounttown and around to Rochestown Avenue. The occasional 46A snaked around the little houses. There was a soccer match at TEK. The shouts from the field, the lazy Sunday bus, brought Sundrive sharply back, memory's force confirming loss's permanence. Then, later, bed: awake, unable to get warm.

Usually, Da dropped me off where Adelaide Road met the top of Harcourt Street, while he took the South Circular on to school in Inchicore. But that Monday he had to return a speaker to the Film Society and asked me to give him a hand. Of course I should have said I didn't want to, that I'd rather walk to work from Suffolk Street, fortified by the bus's companionable cigarette smoke, than have the silent ride conveniently with him. But as usual I said nothing. He could ask whatever he liked – even if it was to leave him. I could take it. (I had taken it, I thought.) Whatever he said had to be treated just like the most trivial request ('Run upstairs for my fags'), because if ever I let on that there was more to it, if ever I revealed that I was not stone, there was no telling what might happen, emotion being bad news since I'd arrived.

It had to be the Film Society, of course; the coincidence is too obvious to be anything but true. While he attended to some paperwork I stood at the office window once again. Confident pigeons still milled around the back of Clery's. Traffic's hoarse susurrus rose to me, as ever – the old, incessant, rustling voice of promise. There was a life out there – even if I didn't have it – in the dispersing mist; and down on the street inaudible, comradely morning calls of strangers. The day before I had become one of those strangers. No tears. Whatever else, no tears! Thus on we rode, locked in our sterile norms. To do other would be to express priority and choice, as though we thought each other people rather than images. Better that than being a familiar treated strangely. I took what I knew would be a last look around. Sundrive gone. North Earl Street going.

'Ready?' We turned to leave.

'Look,' said Da. 'I'm sorry I shouted at you yesterday.'

I'm sorry . . . ! But he'd never spoken so intimately to me. And I did look. Now! I heard my heart say. Tell him. Better yet, listen, let him tell you. It's the last minute of the eleventh hour. He's going to say, let's start again, let's pretend it never happened, you'll be going to UCD in the autumn – here, I brought you the scarf; we're all going to America in the summer, for good, I have a job at Frankie Avalon High, the Bronx – no, no; it's a long way from Boston. Would you like an electric guitar? No? A set of drums? C'mon, we'll go to Pigott's now. It's okay. I'll take the day off. Have you ever been in UCD? C'mon. Don't worry about Peg. I'll 'phone her . . . The city seemed to withdraw.

There was only silence, our own special medium.

'Aw, it's okay,' I muttered. My valedictory to childhood.

The 15 to Harcourt Street was empty. The river stank the same as ever. The man with the tall white hat was in the window of the Westmoreland Street Bewley's raking the coffee-beans in the pan of the machine that also helped Dublin smell like Dublin. I got off at the Standard, crossed over, went in.

'Oh Peg,' I said, and then at last the tears came gladly down.

But the hardest part was still to come. Still snivelling, I made my case: if I could have an extra five shillings a week I was sure I could afford digs. Would she . . . ? Could I . . . ? Peg said she'd have to ask: meanwhile I should wash my face and run out to the Monument Creamery in Camden Street for scones for the elevenses; there was a good lad.

The following Friday I got my four pounds five. Freedom! Soon afterwards, Peg found me digs – in Rathmines, no less, where digs were supposed to be. Maybe things would turn out right after all. Peg came out to Monkstown to collect me and the bag and drove me over to Mrs Luby's – back to where she had shown me my nation's tricolour – green/amber/red – at the lights by the Stella, preferring to stand in the exhaust fumes than to spend the whole afternoon visiting Peace in Leinster Square, exhibiting her first-born. Buses in Rathmines; our earliest memories of being in Dublin together. So it was possible to start over; it was possible to back to a Peg-and-I world. One childhood went, another was reclaimed.

She parked a little down the road in Monkstown but needn't have. Nobody was in.

And so I left my father's house.

There have been other dreams. Of course. But Da was the prompt and pretext of the earliest, least forgettable ones.

He was the man whose hand I held as we walked the iron roads at Christmastime around Lismore. He was the man of words, from whom I learned the names of trees – the sycamore, the silver birch – in summer sauntering through   51

Jacob's Wood. 'As I was sittin' by the fire / Atin' spuds 'n drinkin' pohrter': that was one of the songs he taught me. And when 'The One-Eyed Reilly' was frowned upon in Swiss Cottage, I felt glad inside because that only drew me nearer to Dublin. He was a story-teller: 'Once upon a time there were two men. One was called Lennie and the other George . . . . '

'But what about the mice?' I asked, after the unhappy ending.

'Oh . . . . ' And with his marvellous combination of eagerness and patience (what a teacher he must have been!), he tried to explain that in this case mice didn't really mean mice – well, it meant mice, all right, but not *mice*. I took his word for it, but sighed, preferring my Beatrix Potter straight.

In Sundrive Road he stuffed an old sock full of newspaper, put three sticks against the rear wall of the house and called for cricket. I with a hurley, carved his errant yorkers through the covers, which the lupins going to seed patrolled. My name was Basil Butcher. He was Typhoon Tyson. He used to imitate the wireless, making me guffaw and lose my wicket with his backward square leg and silly mid-on. When rain stopped play he would take down the Britannica and show me that Rex Alston wasn't joking: you really could invent a deep third man if you wanted him. What a quaint game, with most positions *ad hoc*, not to mention lunch, tea, and a round field. It was true: the English were the men for oddity. There seemed a freedom in it. I regaled Mam with all I learned. She said that it was oul shoneens who played cricket now: in her day when only gentlemen wielded willow, Lismore beat the Australians (Mam voted for Dev but it was in the style of the masters he supplanted that she'd been formed and which she upheld as right, visiting a moral *droit de seigneur* on her dependents, like a Kipling character, a potent mix of mixed signals).

Da stayed a playmate for as long as he could. He tried to evolve from being a playmate into being a good sort. Though as far as I was concerned boarding-school was a bad idea – particularly compared with such attractive and convenient alternatives as Synge Street, or Drimnagh Castle, plus a life together – he tried to take the sting out of it. He didn't give me hell for getting 0 in geometry (no marks, that is: zero!) from Barney in the 3B Christmas exam. I remember being

dumbfounded when Bogman, one of the Lord's anointed,

got particularly riled one day at my being blinded by terror to his pedagogical accomplishments (he was a fully paid-up member of the shout-and-knout method) and roared that I was nothing but a lazy little caffler and if I told that to my father would he write to complain about it too. But I never did find out what he'd complained about (wouldn't ask, wasn't told).

Even one of the dreaded conversations of teenage – the man-to-man, what-are-you-going-to-be one – didn't go too badly. It took place one day we spent at Monkstown, clearing builders' rubble from the front yard. He had just bought the house; the wedding was coming up. The job was not my idea of a good time, but I thought of it as an investment – in years to come I'd be able to lie on the lawn for which we were now preparing. The talk turned to me during the tea break, as we played under the splendid oak in the front. Ticking off, turn and turn about, the large number of occupations I was unfit for did not take very long. 'The Guards. The Army. Aer Lingus.' I waited for the Bank and Civil Service to give Da his due, but he didn't bring them up. 'I suppose the Church doesn't attract you?' he said. No, Christ! 'Well what would you like to do?' I said, 'I'd like to go to University.' But there was no money for that. Houses were dear; weddings, too, no doubt. So that was that. We filled more barrowloads of stones. Then, he asked me endearingly, at teatime, if I'd ever seen *The Magnificent Seven*? No? Well, it was on at the Ormond, Stillorgan: if we hurried. We flung aside the cups and plates, like undomesticated boys, and ran.

Mild air, tinged with salt, steamed from the darkness through the open upstairs windows of the 46A. I was still tingling from the evil Eli Wallach (Da told me his name) going 'Khwhy?' with a twist of his mad face. I practised silently saying the name Horst Bucholz. After a while I ventured, 'Da, is that the best Western ever made?' He spoke in that familiar, so reassuring, even interested way. *Stagecoach*, he thought, was the best. And had I ever heard of *The Seven Samurai*? I should see that if I got a chance. Japanese, samurai; history, you see, that makes a difference – there's a story and there's a bigger story behind it, not like in Westerns, although of course, Ford, *She Wore a Yellow Ribbon* . . . . ; *Rashomon*, that was another good one. It was like old times, that last night out   53 we had together, him telling me stories.

But the playing and the fellowship stopped. They would have had to, in any case, I suppose (though why?). Too bad that more insidious games supplanted them, though, and that they ended when they did. Da might have become more than a handful of impressions, more than the fabulous absentee, more than the longed-for solution who became perplexing silence. That morning Morris Minor could have been a UCD for me. I might have learned that fathers are not only parents but are also agents of time and perpetrators of meaning, our fateful precursors, possessors of, participants in, the bigger picture; verbs in the life sentence. Da could have told me how things were with An Fear Mór and the Irish College at Ring, to which when he was my age he used so often to cycle, and why. What about the time at Croke Park when, during half-time with Dev present, teachers ran out onto the pitch protesting and had the stuffing beat out of them by the Guards? Was that during the '46 strike? And what did he do when the strike was on? He might have told me who Frank Edwards was, and how he got to know him. It never happened. Instead we had the puttering of the car for company. That Morris Minor was our hearse. It was what the black pram of Sundrive became when it grew up.

But it was only after his funeral, and in opposition to the hostile voices' final fling, that he became the alternative reality I'd sought. I was told what a 'bloody fool' he was, him with his BA and HDip, not even ending up a school inspector, when probably the whole Department was open to him ('he was a fluent Irish speaker, you know'), and with it entry to every bishop's parlour in the country. In other words, the years at St Michael's Primary – virtually his whole working life, that is – were put in because he didn't know how to be ambitious, not because he might have had different ambitions quite at odds, perhaps (let's hope), with the *status quo*, a way of professional life which may have, in its very absence of conventional getting on, expressed rejection of the state's numerous clerisies. 'And what about the time he was offered the job with UNESCO in Spain? But oh no – he wouldn't live in Spain for God nor man. Him and his principles. He'd make you sick.' Oh, the sin of self! The malevolent eccentricity of choosing not

54

to be dictated to . . . .

'And you know he was a terrible Red. Oh he was, yeah. He was years out of training college before he could get a steady job. Rathcormack? No, he was only subbing there. Then he was some place in Carlow for a while. Carlow! What brought him up there God only knows. But that's the truth: a Jam in trousers, that's what he was for years.' (A Jam, Junior Assistant Mistress, the staff of teaching life for many poor-paying convent schools, was the lowest form of existence in a browbeaten profession.) 'That's where being a Red got him. But you may be sure he's paying for it now . . . . Remember this, Seoirse: the Catholic religion is a hard one to live in, but a grand one to die in. Did you know he was after teaching himself Russian?'

Oh my God, he had a history. He hadn't spent his whole life bogged down in life's abysmal privacy, with widows and spinsters on the one hand, Christian Brothers on the other. He ultimately proved himself the family's version of a fifth columnist not just by what he did – or, in the voices' terms, failed to do – but by what he thought. Ingrate, liberated son of Cathleen ní Houlihan's husband, *patria o muerte*. I hope he was a Red. And kept his head. And had his happy family, too, at last.

Four people on a beach. It's in the Hampton's at Slea Head, near Quiberon. There are two little girls, playing with each other, not playing with each other, present, simply, like ponies in a paddock. The wife and mother walks briskly ahead by herself. On the edge of things, in shirt sleeves and bare feet, a middle-aged man of average height and build. Wavelets of surf tickle his toes. His face is as brown as a walnut: the weather's been great. The scene has great weather's radiance. Every so often, Da gazes up into the serene sky, peers out over the glinting, mercurial sea, as though he's seen something. It's just a habit: there's nothing there but sea and sky. There's nothing to distract. No backward looks. I see that everything here combines the uncanny closeness of a painting with a painting's uncanny distance. I see that this picture is the offspring of the mother-and-child in the off-limits parlour. Then Da resumes the serious business of eating an ice-cream.

II
BOY WANTED

The earpieces had to be highly polished for the sake both of presentability and painlessness of fit, and in order to achieve the height of gloss required, the brushes of the electric polisher – the coarse brushes for the initial, clarifying shine; not the buffers (Great God! was there no end to the variety of things?) – had to be loaded with a porridge of pumice powder and oil. In which I, and everything around me, regularly took a shower.

But to get the earpieces into polishable condition the surplus plastic had to be hewn from them, which required the application of different size bits in the electric drill – one would never do, oh no. The bits were always getting stuck in the drill-shaft, and I invariably grabbed them panicking: now look at what I was after breaking: therefore a regular feature of the daily grind was those buggers of bits trying to roast my fingerprints off.

So that the earpieces reach a hewable state, the plastic moulds had to be boiled. I never remembered to set the time. When the moulds were boiled they had to be extracted from the casts. It was most important to hit clearly the pins holding the two halves of the casts together. Otherwise, if dented, the pressure wouldn't work properly or something, and pressure was everything. Guess what I did? And when it came to mixing the plaster in which to set the wax impression of the client's ear in order to make the mould for the plastic to go into prior to boiling in the cast, so that eventually these would be things of hew and grind – well, there is a house in Harcourt Street which has some unique abortive *putti* and traces of moulding on the ceiling of one room which unaccountably escaped the eye of C. P. Curran.

59

Ah, if only Da could have seen me whipping up a storm of plaster – those foaming peaks, those gobs in the eye! – he would have thanked (might even have paid) me for being such a disenchanted stoker. If I had been as eager to please him as I was to satisfy my boss and benefactor, Mr Franz, the Monkstown home would have been ashes in no time. Stoking had been surprisingly good job-training. It had taught me that the one way to demonstrate discharge of responsibilities was to make dirt energetically. Impress through mess. And I had to impress: I had to act as though there was a future here. The International Electronic Company – meaning Mr Franz and Peg, though they had a sleeping partner, a man with a turnip face and an office in South Frederick Street – was all I had to cling to. Thus, cling I must, quoth Handy Andy, son of Uncle Podger.

Securing and validating my grip were my high hopes. I was doing well, wasn't I? At least I was not out in the mountains lectoring, exorcizing and portering with bekirtled former schoolmates, seminarians at Ballyboden. I wasn't in a muck sweat wondering if I'd got the Junior Ex. or not. I didn't have to wear a uniform; the brown coat, identical to the ones worn by Billy Power and Paddy Flynn in the Co-op in Lismore, didn't count, since I was no shop assistant. I wasn't even serving my time. A trainee, that's what I was. Besides, instead of the banality of a brown coat, what I wore was a robe of plaster-and-pumice cake-mix, modelling my work's image of itself. Looking the part, even if I couldn't play it, made me feel happy (though Peg complained about the cleaning bills). I was something in the city.

There were drawbacks, of course. Being merely a trainee I had to go to school. Go back: that was a bitter blow. But it would be at night: that was exciting. But it would be Kevin Street, the Tech: that was humiliating. Tech had analphabetic connotations. Tech was cousin-german to Manual, and to the kind of boys that were continually wanted in the evening papers – those cramped, pictureless columns containing nothing but the most urgent and anonymous kinds of news: the stark, ungraphic format that I only knew from death notices. I never thought I'd be so near to them. I tried not to think about it. The word 'trainee' helped, also 'international' and 'electronic'. Words were useful, definitely: they kept

60

reality at bay. Reality was silence. That was the worst. Faces blotched and puffy in the aftermath of insult. Necropolitan avenues of want-ads.

Another very helpful word was 'salary'. It made four pounds a week sound a lot more than it was. Thanks to it, I already heard myself among the professionals. And, as I was told and half-believed, I wouldn't feel the time passing until I was qualified (another wonderful word); all my tomorrows a sea of jam. I too would drive a Fiat 1800, like Franz: yes, the day would come when I'd take the bus only for old times' sake. I just had to look at Peg: for years she'd worked for half-nothing. Now she was a company director, name on the letterhead and everything. And she was only a woman. There-fore, I had no trouble seeing myself quit of brown coats, not to mention the combined gradgrindery of vindictive machinery and Tech. I saw the life in a suit, on the phone, Peter Stuyvesant in hand, and *Take a letter, Miss McGonigle. Dear Sirs. Thank you for the favour of yours of the 20th ult?* That was the style.

Better yet. *Sehr geehrter Herr*, and by all means, *Mit freundlichen Grüssen . . . .* For we certainly were international. In a year or two I would be off perhaps to Erlangen to learn the secrets of the dB and the diode from Siemens, the smartest people in the world, whose hearing-aids we sold and serviced. I would be quite safe: Bavaria was Catholic. Not like Crawley New Town where Acusticon, our American brand, had their plant. Still, I might be old enough to look after myself by then. And if I really showed promise, there might be a trip to Sheffield to don the modern halo of earphones and see the Peters Audiometer people do their stuff. That white noise was amazing. And I'd be one of the few people in Ireland to have ever heard of it, that static which sounds like the death-rattle of nature.

Yes, and not merely international but electronic as well. See: I couldn't have been more modern if I tried. And I didn't have to try: here it was, laid on like the gas – safe, secret, instantane-ous. Electronic: the sex in the head of electricity. Those *luidín*-sized hearing-aids that the clients from Booterstown and Rathgar liked so well were only the start of things. Soon they would be – I could see – no bigger than the Smartie-sized batteries that now drove them. Hearing-aids as earrings, as brooches; barettes as bone-conductors. The designers of the 61 fake-spectacle had the right idea. And why stop at ears? I could see a day when there would be electronically-activated false teeth, when instead of hearts there would be batteries. I lay awake at night dreaming of electronically-heated shoes, of duffel coats modelled after electric blankets, their circuit made once toggles all were fastened. If you wired up a *crios* you'd probably make wheelchairs obsolete: arise, switch on thy *crios* and walk. All when I came of electronic age. And why not? Lemass was on the cover of *Time*.

And, as though in support of my fantasies, not to mention being sweet compensation for the travails of Monkstown, there was the honeymoon. Peg, Franz and I did not exactly do the town in my first few weeks with them, when they could still optimistically assume that my splatterings and breakages were just a phase, like pimples. To one but lately liberated from black cabbage and the Argosy variety of potato, however, it certainly seemed that way. I was the missing link, to be styled and polished to fit right in, so that a bright and prosperous future would be had by all.

It began with the razor.

'Do you shave, Seoirse?' Peg asked.

'No. Why?' I was on the point of telling her that I wasn't anywhere near big enough for that yet; sure it was only after I had done the Inter. Cert. for the second time that my oxters started sprouting.

'Well, it's time you did, I think,' said Peg.

'You mean – !' A man – me?!

Peg offered to be my witness and provided the operation's venue. Only she had no shaving tackle (of course – the very idea!), just a miniature plastic yoke for scraping her legs, the blade of which was about as bright as the neophyte to whose face it was about to be applied. There was no lather, either, but Cusson's Imperial Leather provided peak enough. Or so I thought.

'Oh my God! Look at the cut of you! Are you all right?!' Peg shrieked, giggling.

I had circumcized my face. I had made myself my own blood brother. I was a man: the evidence – this grotesque menstruation, a nostril, an earlobe, pimples, chin all redly wept. I 62 ruined two terrycloth towels, which sobered Peg. She recommended electricity from now on.

I agreed: either that, I thought, or the relative safety of a knife and fork. I was embarrassed, but the soothing remedy being proposed – be incompetent, be rewarded (the honeymoon's theme, in effect) – made it all worthwhile. Someone understood me, it appeared.

By chance, the Leaving Cert. results came out soon afterwards, so my honours in Latin and English could be rewarded without it seeming that I was being ridiculously spoiled. But I almost missed getting anything more than a black look, by blithely saying how much I was looking forward to a Philishave – largely because the radio programme for them had Denis Brennan and his wonderful voice. A Philishave would never do: Philips were dirty Jews. Then, having instructed me in truth, Franz led me to a trade-counter in Lower Abbey Street, dealt huffily with the friendly brown-coated counter-hand, and handed me my Siemens (it broke soon after International Electronics and I parted company), a machine which, followed by a visit to the Waldorf, a superior-smelling haircuttery in Westmoreland Street basement, made me a presentable dining-out companion.

The Moira. Interior dim, sophistication's shade. In that lobby it was always five on a mild September afternoon. Cigar aroma; gentle, unpressing telephone bells. Double Century, Noilly Prat, Dubonnet: the vocabulary of pleasure. I watched, careful that my eye and jaw retain their usual extensions. Quiet Trinity Street bereft now of insurance drones; a shortcut into Dame Street. But the shortcut was an end in itself – oh, skittish city!

They know the barman: 'Vincent, *s'il vous plaît.*' Vincent serves. He's liked. He knows his place. He tinkers with the glasses, with the cordials and *digestifs*, those ambers and amethysts, liquid birthstones, unfolders of destinies. No paper-sellers here; no traffic. We raise our glasses. 'Chin,' says Peg, adding a hearty, 'sir'. I drown my obsequious grin in a Club Orange. And to follow, rainbow trout. I have to wait and see what the lemon is for, and the strange knife. Apple pie *à la mode*: more meltings. Franz knocks back a Cognac, proffers a tawny note. '*Allez . . .* '

And then the big test came. The lake, the boat, the day's fishing at Carrickmacross. If I pleased Franz here – as Peg had done: she'd been a number of times – all would certainly keep on going as merrily as a wedding bell. But even before we left town that Saturday morning I knew the day was going to be a washout. I had tried to protest that I knew nothing about fishing – a mistake, since it merely revealed me to be exactly what the occasion required, an emptiness to be filled. Peg told me with loving reassurance that there was nothing to it – look at her, she'd picked it up in no time. 'Ja, ja,' Franz corroborated proudly. And then he launched into what he'd taught her. Peg said, 'Oh, he did: he's a great teacher.' But what if someone – a hypothetical case, of course: myself – detested the whole idea of fishing, considered it a distillation not a sublimation of the tedium that is country life? But how could anyone, not to mention anybody Irish, even think along non-fishing lines. They had me hooked: I couldn't not be Irish, so I kept my mouth shut. But what, I thought, if I'm being roped in not just to the day but into others' dreams, and perhaps not dreams that they could pay for, that sharply took me in as I observed the hefty tip for Vincent. What if I was their future much more than they were mine, more investment than person? Yet, they seemed kind, the way they made a present of the present, forgiving blunders. And later (the promise was implicit) I would have a present of my own. The dream of Dublin lived, I told myself, hoping I'd be able to believe it.

Boring Meath and boring drumlins; lake like a boring sheet of steel. And it was cold too in the damn boat: too soon the splendid coffee was all gone. I put in my usual day's work, stabbing myself with the hook, casting into the rushes, half of me Laurel and the other Hardy ('a fine mess you've gotten us into'), impatience gnawing at me like a piranha. And of course a stupid fish permitted me to catch him; distressing me with the purity of his panic (*mon semblable – mon frére!*). Get back, you naked thing! I wrenched the hook ineptly from his pouting lip and crudely fired him back, as far as he would go. Now there was blood all over my fingers (shag this for sport, anyway!).

And whether it was the extraordinary lifelike quality of the blood – it seems that I'd been expecting, if anything, something like the wake of snails, silvery and thin, as though fish were nothing but slivers of tender rainbow; whether I was in that hypnotic state on the other side of cold and boredom, or subconsciously needed to retaliate against Franz's cheery commendation of my success (till then he'd been seated in the prow with his back to me, reeling in with tiresome regularity quivering entities he called disparagingly 'rutt' and 'brim' – nothing apparently was going to satisfy him but perch, if possible the best and biggest perch in Monaghan. In Ireland. Ever. I blanched to see up close the sportsman's solitary greed) - in any case I discovered after a while that I had done – perpetrated the very thing that above all – and I had Franz's frequent, solemn and pedantic word on this – was a piscatorial horror and abomination.

A mare's nest. That's what he called it, anyway – I know no other name – from that day to this my rod has remained downed and – apostles and fellow-countrymen forgive me! – I have abhorred fishing as nothing more than grotesque underwater golf. A mare's nest was a getting of one's line in an inextricable tangle around the reel. I have no more idea how it came about than I have of how I hooked my misfortunate fish. Had I had sense, I would have let the line dangle in the water all day long and dreamt of pleasanter things. But an image had been proposed for me, and who was I to reject it? No wonder things got in a twist. So an hour or more was spent hacking and picking at the horrible knot. The air was filled with clots of Flemish, the splendid, oathy sound of which was the day's one bright spot, joke-vivid, though of course I didn't dare laugh. Franz threw the pliers and the knife from him enraged. Great stuff! – see, he could act the child as well. Better still, when at last the last hank of severed line had been cast into the lake, Franz peremptorily deemed the light too poor to go on fishing, and he drove like a madman, in a blazing silence, back to town. We were home before dark. The grey quays looked beautiful. Who could ask for anything more?

'Ye're early,' Peg said, carefully scanning our faces. 'How did ye do?' Franz made an immense Gallic shrug and poured himself a Tio Pepe. 'Catch anything, Seoirse?' Oh just the usual, I said silently, with a forlorn, self-pitying look: boredom, anticlimax, fear, embarrassment, futility – and probably a cold. Yet, I vaguely felt that somehow that was not the whole story.

'*Georges*, come once!' Franz peremptorily barked.

'Come at once' is what he meant, so I automatically went, 'Right, sir!' *Shit*, what is it now? As if it made any difference. It was only that I had broken something, burned something (my range with the soldering iron was awesome), forgotten something. And it was only to Franz that any of it made a difference.

The honeymoon was over.

It would have ended anyhow, of course. The year was closing-in, there would be no more fishing, Tech had started; all good things must come to an end. Even I knew that life could not consist of a series of appointments with a fish-slice at the Moira. And the Carrickmacross débâcle had some fall-out – nothing vindictive, mind; no ridicule; merely more frequent mutterings in Flemish, more expansive, resignatory shrugs. The fishing trip had undoubtedly confirmed the early intimations: I really wasn't all that smart – not a patch on Peg; certainly nothing like himself. Was I perhaps becoming an unforeseen problem? A ticklish question. But the Tech might answer it. Softly, softly, catchee monkey . . . . Yet I sensed Franz was having uncharitable second thoughts about where his charity to me was getting him.

For my part, the best I could do was make my 'sir' sound cheerful and obliging, sensing that politeness would protect me from the depredations of my hands. 'Sir' was a good word; it bespoke a sense of self-awareness on the part of the lowly which the high and mighty appreciated. After a thousand repetitions, however, I found myself wanting to experiment a little with its sound and slant. I discovered that by saying it slightly too loud and with quasi-military promptness that I was pleasing myself more than deferring to the boss. All Franz heard was a reasonably accurate echo of what Peg said. He had no need to hear more. His deafness tickled me. Besides, the more I sirred the less I had to use his proper name. This pleased me too. My diminishment in his mind was reciprocated by his in my intonation. If I was turning, he too attained to genre. He was just the boss.

Peg, however, didn't see him like this at all. Her 'sir' was all sincerity; her 'Mr Franz', used interchangeably, was nothing if not fond. To her, it seemed, he was like a friend of the family, a big brother, more welcome in her life than certain relatives. I remember hearing her tell Mam about him, how natural he

66

was, how well he'd done for himself in Ireland. 'There now for you,' Mam said, 'and there's boys down the street in Lismore hardly making a shilling.' (Protracted discussion ensued of the town's most economically moribund – Peg's once prospective beaux? Bottom line and remedy: a good kick up the backside is what they needed.) When Mam and Franz met, he kissed her hand and said '*Madame*', and insisted that she take a glass of Dry Sack. His accent might make him sound like a runaway washing-machine, but he was a gent, all right. And a practising Catholic into the bargain. The combination of classiness and the proper creed was such a rarity in Ireland that it made for tolerance of foreignness. I doubt if Mam or Peg had ever come across such a perfect combination of social and cultural credentials. Any family would be proud to own him – or, if it came to it, to be owned by him. No wonder Franz exuded an air of self-confidence that bordered on the narcissistic. We'd never met a success like him.

To Peg, in particular, I think, Franz was an apparition of the beau-ideal. Not amorously speaking. Franz was much older than her; besides, his wife and children had accompanied him on his *hegira* from Antwerp. But this was the beauty of it. Because he was an older man he could lead by example, he could set the tone, talk to the bank, wrestle with the responsibilities. All Peg had to do was listen and pamper, act the helpmeet and work her fingers to the bone in managing the day-to-day minutiae. Franz knew how to order: she knew how to wash-up. What better ideal to look up to than the engineer-entrepreneur. And an exile, what was more, survivor of 'a tough old time'.

The honeymoon, in Peg's view, was seen, I think, as an apt preliminary to a marriage of true minds between myself and Franz. She probably made a large emotional investment in the happy-ever-after promise of such a liaison. I can remember how she kept encouraging me when Franz got mad, and when I, fearful of a future without her (afraid that the world was only a slot machine – things without people), abjectly apologized for the day's disaster. And sensing perhaps that this marriage, which she'd sponsored, might prove as much a torment to her as the one she so comprehensively disapproved of (and from which she had rescued me – how could I dispute it?), she would talk to me of Franz, what a clever man he was, really;

what guts he had; how he was as honest as the day was long; how he may be hard but he was very fair. 'Stick it out, boy. You'll do all right.'

Franz himself rarely spoke about the past. He might mention Knokke or Louvain with a bland, 'Ja, very nice', meaning for stupid tourists (bloody foreigners), or remind us that, broadly speaking, all Walloons were schtinkers, a judgment he felt all the more entitled to, he implied, because of how we thought of Northerners. But I got nothing from him about Ghent or Aix or I-sprang-to-the-stirrup-and-Joris-and-he, much less about Gheel, the town for madmen founded by our own St Dympna, for which I obscurely imagined Franz, aid to the deaf, might have a feel. Once, reminded by a client's anecdote about outwitting a Guard, he passed some remark about how he used to infuriate the Germans because, although he had his shop in Antwerp, his home was outside the city, in a different jurisdiction, so could refuse their orders to man the rooftops, join the bucket-chain. He seemed nostalgic, just for a moment, then. But why? Peg told me that the war had been wicked. Nights of bombs. The port burning, the sky burning. They had no coffee, just some kind of chicory juice. So that was why he came to Ireland: it was bilingual, and we had Irel – a liquid to make coffee from that looked like a glutinous version of California Syrup of Figs. And as to what memory might wash up, there was no telling, as I knew.

It struck me as odd though that, having survived the war, Franz didn't stay home to enjoy the peace. When I asked about this, Peg, usually so good at telling all, grew vague; it was something to do with things after the war, a new Antwerp government. Politics – boring, weren't they? But (Peg hurried on) he loved Ireland. And wasn't it great, the way he built himself up? He didn't know a sinner here, couldn't even speak English. But he stuck to it. That's what the country needed, men like him. Modern, go-ahead. When you think of how well he's done, it really shows us up. A few more like him, now, and we'd be on the pig's back.

Peg was right. Franz was the Marshall Plan, the technological revolution, the signpost to rainbow trout and snazzy cars, enhancer of our neutral peace, creator of opportunity, master of plastic, terminator of the fifties. (Pray for us! Have mercy on us!) I had so much to be grateful for . . . I was lucky, really, say what I like. Mr Franz might be hard, but y'know, it's a hard oul life, it's a trial. I did know indeed: he grabbed the drill, the spatula, from my hand, 'No; hold it so. So! *Gott verdamme . . . . '* It was for my own good, really, he'd make a man of me. (He owned the spatula. He owned the way to hold the spatula. I had to let him. Could I stop him? Who had a better right than he, after all? – in business for himself.

It all made sense. My problem was that the kind of sense it made did not appeal to me. It was a sense that placed one man on a pedestal. Franz was the triumph of the will, the machine rampant with quids sinister, with (for all I knew) any amount of devices at his disposal, with all of which I would be required to identify in due course. Whether it was all too modern for me (dreams notwithstanding), or whether it was because there once was a man in Monkstown whom I wanted to be and when that didn't work I declined a substitute, or whether it was something simple like knowing I couldn't get on with a man who apparently had no stories, it came to the point that when he bent over to inspect or direct what I was doing I felt strong urges to hit him with a hammer on his perfectly bald brown egg of a head. And I laughed to myself. Because I realized that, no matter what else, I was not like him – I was free to be unlike him. Was that what my inchoate post-Carrickmacross feeling of not-quite-total despondency meant? Such thoughts – the first ones of my own I can remember having – made me feel slightly giddy, the same way I felt before going on a journey.

2

But even if I'd been in the shed at home with Georgie I would have had some of the same problems, since over and above the matter of personality – all-consuming as it was to approval-needing me – there was the more basic matter (which the press of personality squeezed aside) of work, the application of self to world, the expenditure of energy and the consumption of materials (the subjugation of the fish). The sheer externality of all that was an immense strangeness to me – quite apart from the fact that this was to be done for someone, at the behest of a stranger. That strangeness never went away, and was a more unnerving source of my unhappiness than the Franz-tension, since it bore out all I had been told about my uselessness, and all that recent experiences were giving me to understand about life's essential autism.

No doubt there were aspects of what I did which exacerbated this hypersensitivity – often I was struck, in the back room at Harcourt Street, in the space between the noise of one activity and the next, of how reminiscent my self-consciousness was of the way I used to feel, as a child, in the midst of adults when they talked politics, say, or mentioned unfamiliar names (Casement, Amritsar). The materials and machines had the same vividness and impermeability. They were more specific, they possessed greater gravity and density than I felt, and believed, I did. They cost more.

Being in the back didn't help, of course. The back windows looked out on nothing: the windows in the front had 48As to Ballinteer pass by them, 62s to Goatstown. The phone was in the front. And along with Peg, there was always a secretary to talk to, a fairly rapid succession of nice girls – three in less than the two years I was there – with whom it was difficult to be properly friendly but who at least were reminders that there were aspects of the life to come that no employer need provide for. It felt lonesome sitting at the bench, oblivious until it was too late of the drill racing on its appointed rounds, mindful of nothing but the silence within me. The feelings of lonesomeness, of being less deprived than unworthy of the front because of my position (eloquently communicated by the state of my brown coat), were intermittent, however, and probably insinuated themselves when other aspects of the job were getting me down. One thing that really gnawed at me was the repetition. It was nothing except boil and grind the whole time I was there. The earpieces had names – Mr Stott, Mrs Cargill – but they seldom had faces. I was either going somewhere at an excruciatingly low rate, or getting nowhere very quickly.

But then work itself was appalling. Even more than by the conditions and character of the job, my feelings of defeat and nonentity and fearful loathing were brought on by a vision I developed of work in general. I couldn't bear the smallness of it. The minute but crucial differences that constantly occurred provided me with a distressing climax to adolescence – the general impossibility of everything. If the powder and water were not whipped together into a consistent creamy porridge, air bubbles could get trapped, causing the plaster – in which the precious earpiece-in-the-making was encased – to split when boiling under pressure. (I knew how it felt: one air-bubble could definitely ruin your whole day.) If the plastic dough to be inserted in the earpiece mould hadn't set properly, the earpiece, after boiling, would be opaque, hence visible, hence potentially embarrassing to the client. Overea-gerness with sandpaper could result in a minute looseness of the piece in the client's canal and the shrieking torment of feedback. I couldn't tolerate the notion of a world in which significance had so minute a sphere of operation, in which ratification or occlusion of self was balanced on the slender fulcrum of such tolerances. When I thought of the world – which I did a lot, since I didn't seem to be living in it, quite – I thought of sums of parts, not parts themselves. I thought of worlds within the world – books, films, cities, girls. Bubbles and dust were not my style. And there was the matter of pace, too. To work with smallness, I found, was to work slow; to work as if there were world enough and time, and that the task in hand exerted a proprietary interest over time and world. But I was seventeen-eighteen-nineteen. I didn't want time, I wanted speed. I wanted to be on my bus.

So I was a failed machine. A bored failed machine, at that. From pure forgetfulness I branded a new sheet of bakelite with the soldering iron – 'These things cost money!' 'Seoirse, how could you?' One day, no reason at all, I stuck a screw-driver into a socket on the main plug board. There was a little pop and a bluish-yellow flash, that was all. Typical, I thought: even my involuntary but evidently incurable anarchism lacked force and spectacle. A little later I heard Franz shouting at a client, then the dry hiccup of switches. Nothing worked. Franz flew out of the testing-room and towered above me: 'So!' A coal-chute of Flemish descended. Peg, vigilant of image, rushed back, rapidly shutting the testing-room's various doors, hushing, placating. 'Sure he didn't know any 71 better, sir.' 'For this we pay Tech! *Dumkopf* . . . . ' And later, much less enjoyable, a ponderous homily on the wrongness of not telling – though, digesting this, I made the agreeable discovery that secrecy was a large part of the pleasure; secrecy was always unsuspected; secrecy was something from which I could not be parted. It wasn't long before, noticing how much insulating tape there was, I was taping books inside the lavatory cistern. Many's the sweet Gold Leaf I had in the jax at the end of the hall, relishing the latest hit, *To Kill a Mockingbird*.

The afternoon of the power-cut must also have made a rare impression on the abandoned client. He must have heard some of the shouting. He probably considered us a branch of Lourdes: a foreigner asked you to take a seat, the next you heard voices. Mr Franz the thaumaturge. 'German, is he?' clients would ask hopefully.

As far as I could tell, there were three types of client. The premier class consisted of referrals from Fitzwilliam Square, where, to selected and select consulting-rooms, at Christmas time, I delivered long bottles in interesting oblong boxes, tastefully wrapped. These clients belonged to Monkstown and its familiars, Orwell Road, Nutley Park, Clontarf Avenue. Not all of them were old, either; it surprised me that people in their twenties – their teens, even – lived at such addresses. Some of them were pretty girls my own age, limbs beginning to stretch and frames to fill, now, with all that tennis, all the riding lessons. On Saturday we opened until lunchtime to receive their orders for batteries. I answered the door on Saturdays: Miss Houlihan, the typist I remember best, had the day off – was, even as we sold, still a little gaga from Friday night at the Four Ps (fine for her). But please God it would be Miss Brophy from Booterstown with the sunglasses and the great legs (all Dublin dames had great legs), or Miss Brennan of Clonskeagh – still at school, just right: how about a few tips for the Leaving, Miss – this is a man of the world speaking – interesting you should mention the Babylonian Captivity, I was just thinking there the other day, if you ask me it'd make a smashing picture. *Ben Hur* – exactly! Did you like it? I liked Ben, hated her. Sometimes it would be them, but once I started to decoke the throat, they just looked me up and down severely and swept on by into reception. They could hear now; they didn't any longer have to smile when someone wanted to talk to them. Old McMullan, a commercial traveller with a Northern accent, was friendly, a good bit of gas – but who the hell asked *him*?

Other clients – the second class – came up from the country, nuns who'd come into a bit of a legacy, gristled parties with land outside Granard, steered by mannish daughters in suits of navy-blue. The watchful Daddy tried to look more helpless than he was, while daughter simpered. This was her day, really. She'd been at him for years. Deafness was not the will of God (he needn't give her that). It wasn't even natural. Didn't they have machines now above in Dublin, no bigger than a terrier's mickey (God forgive her) some of 'em. And they wouldn't hurt you at all: they do be qualified men. Back home with James she'd get herself into a state: 'Th'oul fecker: he have it all right only he's afraid to part with it. Sure will you ever forget what he gave Pascal for his confirmation? – one lousy two bob!' But now, at last, she had her day in Dublin. The foreign doctoring would soon be done; then tea at Wynn's to watch the priests.

Franz always officiated in such cases. Often, however, they defeated him. 'What?' he'd be heard to exclaim, 'you can't hear *that*?' With the audiometer's testing pitch up full it had an impact on the ears comparable to what my sinuses suffered from the Monkstown fridge. No answer. Then Franz, incredulous, a little disgusted, and totally unaware of what the victory meant to the testee, would declare, a brusque shrug in his tone, 'Then I'm sorry, I can't hallop you.'

'What's tha' fella saying, Mary Ellen?' from the victor.

'Miss O'Brien, come once': Franz on the intercom.

'Sorry, now,' from Mary Ellen, tamely.

Peg, brightly: 'Not at all, not at all. Safe home.'

But *mutter mutter*, both of them, over restorative tea. Another sale gone west.

A much more regular source of income than canny culchies was the Dublin Health Authority. It paid for aid to deaf children. Every so often Franz and I swept out to Cabra or Our Lady's Hospital for Sick Children, Crumlin, in the 1800 – he the Flying Doctor, I trying to play the part of plucky Tommy O'Donnell calling Wolamboola Base. We also went to a school in Ballyfermot. I was afraid, of course.

I was afraid of the world's blight, of nature's blind mistakes, of the schools' trapped smells of drains and cabbage, and the hospital's air of imminence (the worst has not yet happened; it's still imaginable . . .). The little boys had big black boots, grey ganzies, trousers that seemed patterned after chimney-pots. They reminded me of the inmates of the orphanage in Cappoquin, whom we would see being marched out two-by-two as we strolled onto the hurling field. When I whined I was reminded that I didn't know how well off I was – think of the orphans.

It wasn't whining that occurred to me now, but tears. The poverty. The waste. The unbright schoolrooms in outdated premises. The patient nuns, their lives a wishful, imprecise, disturbing mimicry of their charges. The little cross-eyed boy who wouldn't stay still. The passive, downcast little girl with auburn hair and green in her nostrils. Formless utterances and stammering: a kind of incontinent excitement at the visitors, wiring them for life. The vale of tears and Adam's curse. Electronics.

And above all, what my teenage mind fastened on, appal-led, thinking about these visits – swiftly the Fiat flew back to the place where we imagined we belonged, leaving mere Irish drivers, Morris Minors, limping in its backwash – was that they showed me work. Not my work, or their work, but Work, the universal damnation. The gap between the inchoate and the effort was what everybody must feel, I thought. As Georgie, wherever he was, walked onto where the hole had to be before the building could be raised, or when he prepared the flawed parlour to receive paper, I knew him knowing that strange-ness. Da, not many miles away in Kehoe Square, knew it, staring at perhaps the siblings of our hapless clients, and they stared back expectantly at him, knowing it intuitively themselves but believing that 'Sir', in his sirness, in his apart-ness at the blackboard, might talk them out of it. Their atten-dance in the classroom bore mute witness to an understand-ing that the distance was part of a primary order of things and the talk a secondary consideration. These gaps, these flaws, the silences, the daily essays in recuperation (as precisely unavailing as they are availing), the problematic of progress, the indefiniteness of action: I imagined I saw all that in the faces of deaf children. I can only assume that I was looking for it, or that those marginal kids spoke the language I understood best, the language of emotional impressionability.

Thus, I went on (what a great audience I made), machines are useless. They had to be invented, of course, to distract us from, to override, what I presumed to call the truth of what I'd seen. But all they did, like any mask, was draw attention to what we hoped they would disguise (they even broke). Even money, the most wonderful world-turning invention of the lot, the original electronics, supposedly fabricated to soften the blows, only succeeded in making sure the blows fell on someone else. I was not yet nineteen. My salary was four pounds a week and change. The world was turning out to be chronic bollox, a boarding-school with translucent, shifting walls, full of sow's purses longing to be silk ears . . . .

And how then to proceed, besides, as though a nun, succumbing?

I should have been like Peg. Peg was dutiful, Peg was responsible, the right hand ever-ready and best foot always forward.

She wasn't perfect, mind – at least not by the standards I was raised to. She too had been molested by the city: she relished her Rothman's King-sized, and when it was five-thirty a splash of Cinzano did not go amiss with her. She bought *The Daily Telegraph* throughout the whole of the Profumo affair, read with bulging eyes, and told the jokes about it that were going the Dublin rounds. There was going to be a new marmalade – Keeler's little kip; Mandy Rice-Davies did better business because she gave Green Shield Stamps. Peg used to send the weekly edition of *The Daily Sketch* (the five dailies bound) to Mam. At holiday time they'd evaluate like punters Billy Wallace's chances and the fate of Captain Townsend. Ah, the odd English and their public loving: all that divorce – shocking, really: awful . . . . Weren't they shameless? Weren't they gas? Peg also sent, as regularly as clockwork, the English women's magazines whose gaudy romances, complete with the vapid splendours of the oleographer's art, seemed to mimic those in the sovereign's circle, and which had no connection whatsoever to the much more entertaining items by Mary Grant and Evelyn Home.

But as a worker, Peg was no less than the second coming of The Little Flower. And not just during my time with her, 75 when, after all, she was a director and had had the incentive to invest herself. No; she had always given one hundred percent. After the Inter. she had cycled over to the Tech in Cappoquin and in next to no time was typing and taking shorthand to beat the band. Of course there was little call in Lismore for such accomplishments which, in any case had been polished to such a pitch that Dublin was the only fitting showcase for them – Dublin being a far more desirable venue than that nebulous conurbation, England. But how to place her?

Well, as luck would have it, wasn't Peace just newly married and her husband starting up a business for himself. The very thing. Big sister would be on hand to show Peg the ropes and keep an eye on her (since as sure as God she'd be off dancing as soon as she had a few bob in her pocket). But it was a grand business, too, dealing in perfume and vitamins and related requisites for the MPSI's, while Henry – new boss, new husband – was more or less one of our own, since he was from Mitchelstown. And he could sing grand. On top of which, then, poor John – Nuala (God help us) . . . . So Peg was able to move in to Sundrive Road – sure God doesn't close one door but he opens another – where she cooked and washed and cleaned and applied the Coty before she hit the town.

I assume she had her nylons torn to flitters by stocious salesmen in the National, and that she went in style and in high hope to the Metropole's *thé dansant*, Sunday afternoon. And no doubt there were dates; a drive to The Scalp, Portmarnock, of a starry June-time, hops with loutish medicos at Bective Rangers and at Wanderers, dinner-dances at selected minor golf clubs. Dancehall days and love in Dublin . . . . (Let's hope.) What's certain is that she worked long hours, year in year out, in Liffey Street, stuck behind straw and crates, and in the course of time developed extraordinary skill in wrapping and packing and applying sealing-wax, in balancing petty cash, in keeping a weather-eye on the easy-come easy-go drift of messenger-boys who ferried talcs and unguents to Hamilton Long – no doubt for 'moddom' at Switzer's too; and by no means least in babysitting Peace's growing family, preparing the Mount Merrion home for each new arrival, scrubbing the bathroom while the angel cake rose to perfection in the oven. There never was a thing she was asked to do that Peg wasn't able for. She'd never say no, just roll up her sleeves and pitch

76

in without a second thought. A treasure. A godsend. And all she asked for in return – as far as anybody knew – was to have a fortnight, every third year or so (however long it took to amass enough in the Post Office), sweltering under Nivea in San Sebastian or Riccione – 'God, anything for a bit of sun!' (I hear her still.)

Then one fine day she walked. Oh, the badness of her: the saucy thing: too well off she was . . . . Another breach, another unhealed wound. Once again, silence, the seal and mark of ultimate significance. She'd never said a word; nobody ever suspected how fed up she was, or even that she might have been fed up at all; sure hadn't she been given a life – job, roof, that meant – what more did she want . . . . She wanted the job she'd seen in the *Independent*. She'd discovered that, in the end, independence was as simple as that.

She was an instant and sensational success. Franz had found exactly what he wanted. Peg was obedient and obliging. She supplied the human touch to transactions with often fretful clients, teetering as they were, for the first time in their lives, on the brink of intimate newfangledness (if secret ears were becoming commonplace, somebody, somewhere must have been having the inchoate dream that would one day assume material consequence as the vasectomy). She knew, above all, all the varieties of yes – compliance, endorsement, initiative. They had amounted in her by now to a second nature, a nature which took its lead unasked, from Franz Masterful Male. She was ten times the earpiece-maker that I was – 'and I never taught her,' Franz crowed, praising her, showing me up: 'just learned by watching'. He'd taught her how to do the testing, and here too she performed immaculately. And as for keeping the office in order, the statements and invoices and correspondence and the years of training as a packer in Liffey Street coming in so handy after all . . . . She was a gem, truly. Beyond reproach. Franz relaxed, signed over day-to-day matters to her, schemed for more partners and bigger business, cast his entrepreneurial gaze on me, the all-time pig in a poke.

By the time I came on the scene, then, Peg had made it. Not only that, but she had all the appurtenances of having made it. When Franz plumped for the 1800 he bequeathed his old Fiat 1100 to her, and taught her to drive. She had a fine flat in 77

Garville Avenue. Only the indifferent reception on her TV prevented her from being as made for life as anyone on the Monkstown Road. And sometimes she was. Some autumn Saturday afternoons the wrestling came in as clear as anyone could wish, parodying the old, unfeeling confidence tricks of flesh. 'God, but I'd love to be flogging that Mick McManus!'

I heard again the voice that flayed the Welsh. But things seemed different, somehow. Just my imagination, I suppose, but I saw her present, larger life as a diminishment – the result of the shrinking family context perhaps. The car brought her closer to Lismore, where Mam was on her own. The television lulled and dulled the day's exhaustions: there was no need to go out – but really there was no impetus. Besides, she was so good at what she did old clients dropped by to chat (and that was tiring), so she had a social life, so she was too worn-out to have a social life. And she liked to get an early start to beat the traffic and to catch up with the paperwork.

I had seen people work like this. Her father; her brother, George. They could be absorbed to the point of self-forgetfulness. They could stay late and start early, no clock but their own vitality and interest – a species of profound amusement – to monitor them. But that, to me, was the point: those men were working for themselves, as perhaps did Da when he closed the classroom door. I began to think of Peg as though she couldn't, that all she did had to be placed at the disposal of a self not hers. And here I was, the history that was going to repeat herself. True, some of the details had been moved around, as though to suggest that no, really, this was different: I was getting my turn at the Tech now rather than sooner; the cosmetics angle had broadened and become more subtle. But I too had thought that I should serve in order to acquire a life, only to find that when I had the perfect chance to, I was unable. This was one of the strangest dislocations of all, to find I was unlike Peg, too, of whom I was so fond, who obviously was so fond of me, who had apparently done so well: so irrevocably unlike her.

It's tempting to say now that Peg was so fond of me she tolerated my boredom and disaffection with the job, and as a result of her sensitivity I became a messenger-boy. But that's the kind of tribute sentiment has a habit of neatly, retrospectively, paying to the unforeseen. Peg certainly never viewed me as a messenger-boy. If I was fed up, it was my own fault and good enough for me; besides it was only through accidents and incompetence that my state of mind revealed itself, and these my mentors attributed to a state of non-mind, or stupidity (God be with the days when difficulties were thought of as no more than errors in prefabricated meaning!). So, thinking of myself as a messenger-boy was all my own work, and all my own the pleasure of the image – at once false, since I remained to all appearances Browncoat of many colours, and Trainee; and true, since I regularly was sent on messages. Whatever I was, therefore, I was in disguise. Whatever I did, I had an alternative me not doing it, a me like a suppressed giggle. Messenger was trainee's unboring, declassé twin: trainee was messenger's staid good fortune, the chance he should have wanted but for which he was unable to find the necessary need in himself. And I had glimmerings of enjoying myselves now that I could see life being fuller than I'd previously imagined. I was five again with a fantasy pal – certainly the play element struck me, even if I couldn't afford as yet to concede its childishness. But I also saw in the errand-runner something that everyone around me lacked. I was something that, being unsuspected and only of personal, or least-valued, significance, could not be taken away from me. Apparently, imagination could prompt autonomy: more important at that stage, to my mind, was the sensation of impenitence that freeingly accompanied imagination.

There was a tiny shop in Camden Place: that was a regular place to run out a minute to for Aspirin, milk, fags – the instant needs. It was run by a woman with wispy hair, 'from Wickla' she was, she told me. She had spectacles; she was flusterable in the extreme. How she must have suffered: the shop was so small that two customers filled it. That made it interesting the odd time any of the classy secretaries from Arks were present – china shops among bulls, poor things . . . . What had the poor woman inside the counter done to be cooped up in such small-ness? Perhaps she thought it freedom, compared to Wickla. It was hard to tell by her. She had a habit of lifting back her head when anyone came in, which made her look scared, averse, half-daft – the very way, indeed, that the look made at least one of her customers feel he looked. And she confided in me 79 one day: 'Oh, I do get terrible headaches. But they affect me strange, d'you know? Aye; it's in the legs I have 'em.' As messenger-boy it was possible to be a regular, a party to confidences, known. That was great.

Down to the post office past famous Arks – *The Kennedys of Castleross* was done there: I tried standing unobtrusively by the National Children's Hospital to see if I could spot any of the soap-opera's stars, but no; I was forgetting, these were not like old times: no Alfie Byrne, Noel Purcell. Then a quick dart into the second-hand bookshop, and hurriedly by The Green Tureen, the restaurant where there'd been a murder in the basement – Dublin wit had made a meal of that – to the post office. Back then by Cuffe, Wexford and Montague Streets, with a stop for a chat with the white-garbed grocer in the Wexford Street H. Williams who never failed to remind me that I could do a lot worse these evenings than tune in to Tellidew Simrew. I, still loyal to Peg in my way, politely doubted if the Welsh *bostúns* of Teledu Cymru were any better than the local dittos in Telefís Éireann with its Friday evening prime-time offerings of Boris Karloff. But, fair dues, no, I'd never seen Criss-Cross-Quiz; so no doubt he had a point. Thus we parted friends, the elderly, old-fashioned grocer and I. He was constantly pacing up and down outside the shop, brilliant in white apron over white coat, guardian of the old ways, weather-eye out for encroaching supermarkets – Comiskey's a couple of hundred yards away in Camden Street, had turned itself into a superette, run by a young girl . . . 'There y'are,' he'd say, 'the thin end of the wedge'; mordantly straight-faced.

Quite often I had to go farther afield – sometimes even not on any old messages but on official business, to Radionics in Hatch Street or better yet to Brownlee's, Molesworth Street. It was good to have a walk, to breathe at leisure and at length familiar smells. But I wasn't happy with my destinations. Everybody else but me knew what they were doing there; I just handed over the slip of paper with the order written on it, then the money. There was no use pretending to be a messenger-boy in these stores – they were invariably packed with the real thing. And the camaraderie of the electronic cognoscenti also had me at a loss. I often left the receipt behind ('can't even do a simple message . . . . Honestly, I don't know what you're thinking of at all.').

The best of these official outings was the most regular, over to the Munster and Leinster Bank in Baggot Street every Friday. I was entrusted with the wages cheque, also the weekly 'lodgment', another of those darling words like 'salary' and 'trainee'; I loved the way it seemed to go with the bank's sanctimonious air. Four quid lost its nettling impoverishment for a while. But the best part was the walk across the Green. During those walks it was always sunny (the deaf schools I remembered as being invariably dark, with the baby-pink glow of fluorescent tubes causing a false, excessive warmth to suffuse the dank air). There were always girls in short sleeves lying stretched out alone, or in couples sitting, talking, on the grass, absently plucking at it: he loves me, he loves me not . . . I even felt close to the ducks and the flowers. Sometimes I smiled at a girl if I caught her eye, and it didn't seem to matter too much if she turned her head with a huffy flounce – the familiar, who d'you think you are? But, see, it's not all that important at the moment who . . . aw, come on. The only girls to come on, however, I didn't know how to handle, young-wans from York Street or the flats on Redmond Hill, Lowry-thin, features bleached and drawn, marmalade hair in turquoise curlers, shouting. 'Ay, mis-star, Maggie here sez . . . . ' Then screeching. I tried to smile. I knew it was fun, but I was afraid it wasn't friendly.

And always when I was out, there was the city, motoring along with its muted roar and constant movement. It was closer, now that I was on foot. A bike would have been ideal, of course. I envied the real messenger-boys' way with the traffic, weaving in and out of jams on those special bikes of theirs with the short frames and big caged-in basket out in front. But walking did me fine. I felt I'd grown a little, since I no longer wanted to be looking down the whole time from the top deck. And this way I could drop into Combridge's on the way to Brownlee's, or cross the street to the Eblana to see if there were any new Penguins in while I was supposed to have nothing else in mind besides getting Franz the vile shag and green Rizlas from the civil gent in Kapp and Peterson's (another Friday ritual). Yes, the city was there all the time. I hadn't been giving it very much attention. Now I realized that it served my new perception of myself to perfection. What

81

better confirmation need I have that I was a couple of people than to do one thing while I was supposed to be doing something different. Of course! – as I always had believed it could, Dublin would make me up as I went along.

3

Physics was fine. I had the teaching of Bimbo and Bulganin from boarding-school to stand me, unexpectedly, in good stead. I knew how to cheat so that weight in air equalled weight of water displaced: that way the teacher doing the rounds would leave our group alone. But the calculus crucified me and applied maths turned me into a parallelogram of inertias.

The original idea in sending me to Kevin Street was to make me an AMIEE, an Associate Member of the Institute of Electrical Engineers. Franz might have known that he was misguided in this ambition for me by the difficulty he had in articulating such a mouthful. But his conception of me, and of himself, required that if I was not to have a university degree at least I would have as many letters after my name as possible. Like all conceptions (as I was finding out), this one too was blind to its own capacity for error. I still don't know exactly how someone qualified in industrial electrical engineering was supposed to have contributed to International Electronics. Franz, father of three daughters, didn't have very much experience of the educational system, particularly on the technical side. Perhaps, after all, he did go for the sound of the thing, the poet! As anyone could tell, an Institute sounded a lot more impressive than anything with the populist denomination City and Guilds.

Since the courses, the examining bodies and the qualification awarding institutions all seemed to be English – and reflected the way the energies of working people were boxed into fitters, technicians, improvers, trainees, in order that they might earn union rates and fit in with the employers' designs (a place for everyone and everyone in his place, just like the army, just like the priesthood) – that faith in system which snobbery expresses was probably an inevitable influence on Franz's choice. I had never heard the like, of course, and was at first very vaguely, and later totally, unnerved by the way the exam system, the job system and the work system reproduced themselves so incestuously in each other, and how again, everything was premissed on the slowing down of processes and possibilities into minutiae. Here I was, a career fan of the big picture, trying to learn calculus (relative of Gregory, be thou my guide!). How the foolish commonplaces of mathematical problems – the men in fields, their holes, their productivity – became suddenly endearing. At least they spoke in English, not the foreign symbology of integration and differentiation. This was the very stuff I was wisely kept from attempting for the Leaving – and a couple of months later I was taking it on to get a GCE O-level, the *rite de passage* into the kingdom of AVO. It didn't take me long to learn that I was not going to be numbered among the technocratic cherubim and seraphim, and that, even if I was the last of the breed (for look how modern things were becoming), in the phrase of Brother Murphy long ago, 'Ireland is rearing them yet.' 'Rearing what, sir?' 'Eejits – you eejit!'

Twice a week we sat from seven to nine in a lecture hall with a steep rake and long, well-worn desks, while a young man in a suit named Raymond shouted at us earnestly, nonstop, in a voice of pure Kildysart or, perhaps, Belmullet. There were arias on rates of change and ratios, vectors and forces. It was nice, I suppose, to be at school where nobody was going to beat you, but this was just about the only improvement. Kevin Street Tech, then, was a gloomy place. Red brick baked black, the front door in the far right, always shaded, corner of the bike-littered courtyard. During the day, the atmosphere was no doubt unexceptional, but in the evenings the air seemed grey and dusty, as though suffused by a steady trickle of infinitesimal particles from worn stairs and gouged benches. The house of the future had a strangely entropic air. And we were all tired, trudging in after long days and hasty teas: I felt that too. I knew my classmates were the same as me – we weren't going to school; we were being sent. Large areas of choice were already being forgone: they were forsaking the 83 present in order that the future not forsake them. They came in ties, with Conway Stewarts primed. They were older. They knew the difference this chance would make, that CIE and Pye (Ireland) had not elected them lightly to see the future through. They were on the road from Bluebell. And of course there was nothing for it but constant attendance. Absences were reported to the fee-paying employer, which in my case, at least, would lead to a real fight. Since nothing, to my mind, was worse than open criticism, I attended as regularly as clockwork.

The classes were wakes for messenger-boys, as I could see from the memorials carved into the desks: the names, the execrations against boredom and dislocation. Pats, Shels, remembered fondly from the days when all of life consisted of agonizing over a flighty ball. MUNICH, an acronym remembering the glorious dead – Manchester United Never Intended Coming Home. I declined to make my mark: I had no hankering to be remembered here, or to expend the psychic energy necessary to carving a name with pride (and resentment). Instead, after Raymond's first few numbers had made it all too clear that the best I could do was kill time, I looked around for ways of kindly putting it out of its misery.

A solution was readily to hand: the public library just next door. An excellent place it was – first cousin to the Tech in architecture and appointments but with a wonderful stock. And it was like old times in Lismore, being in love with a library again (attempts to have a library in boarding-school proved abortive: library books ran implicitly against the ethos of such places, since they require quiet time in private to be savoured to the full). So before class on Monday I'd borrow my weekly intellectual nourishment. Raymond Chandler and Peter Cheyney – those asphalt Flauberts – were what my taste ran to at the time, and I found that there was little problem swallowing whole one of their productions every two classes.

One night, however, suffering perhaps from a temporary case of calloused palate, or – more likely – experimenting with the stacks' sightlines to get a more lingering, less obtrusive ogle at my favourite check-out clerk, I found myself holding a book with a shrieking yellow cover. I knew such books: Gollancz published some cracking thrillers. But this was different. This was *The Outsider*, by Colin Wilson. I opened it up. It

84

spoke eloquently of nausea, of the country of the blind. Visionary Russians leapt to the eye; and there were the French again, as unashamed as ever. *Aujourd'hui, maman est morte. Ou peut-être hier, je ne sais pas:* this Meursault sounded like one of the original gas men, all right. I hadn't come across a book that seemed this important since *I Believed*, by Douglas Hyde: we all read that during the retreat, the year before the Leaving. I was so excited by *The Outsider* that I didn't read it in class, but saved it up for bed. Reading Mr Wilson was like being back at those illegal, midnight Hallowe'en parties at school, when we sat around the locker-room telling filthy jokes and smoking, the height of being outrageous. The lads in the book were much the same, really. Life was their dirty joke (how true!). And, just like us, Raskolnikov and company were desperate thinkers, passionately indifferent to respectability, were essentially ineducable: the psychic Unemployed. The fallen, or rather, the falling, were great company, especially with the blustery, ringmasterish way Wilson pushed them around, like the Billy Cotton Band Show, in a way. All of which lounging with intellectual riff-raff and messenger-boys did me no good at all when GCE time came round at year's end; my secret life of reading exposed me then, caused the trouble I'd naively thought could be avoided.

We took the GCEs in a school on the Sandford Road, presumably because exams had to be completed before dark and there wasn't room to accommodate us at our normal venue. I performed disastrously. The lowest grade was H, I think; and I bagged an H-trick. And soon enough the firm saw what I'd done. It was a case of from electric razors to being held by the short-and-curlies in one brief year. The Flemish thunder rolled and rolled. I was given an ultimatum: to say what I intended to do now (my God – a decision!) and how I meant to go about doing it. So I cried. But tears did not move Franz of the stone jaw.

Peg, too, spoke quietly and slowly. I pleaded with her that the material was too hard, and gave graphic examples of what I meant, plus a melodramatic account of my mathematical history ('Barney gave me nought in geometry – honest!'). But this was received as though it was a betrayal of family honour – no O'Brien was that stupid. In desperation, I proposed that Eamon, a fellow-guest of Mrs Luby who was doing a degree in electrical engineering (properly, as I thought) at UCD, had mentioned off-handedly, in his opinion, I'd be better off doing the City and Guilds Radio and TV Servicing course. This proposal made Franz's jaw, if not drop, move. He smiled grimly; aha, he'd thought so, when it came to it, I saw that I had no alternative but to take the future seriously and give it thought – unless I wanted to be walking the streets, that is (though, confusingly, I remembered that I liked walking the streets). 'Very well,' he agreed, with menacing forbearance; 'but remember, this is your last shonse.'

It was not his tone that made me uncomfortable but the realization that he seemed to know me. He had been thinking about me too. Perhaps we differed about the impetus and terminology of his thought. But basically he had me dead to rights. I was afraid to go. I needed International Electronics. I seemed not to be the type who'd murder to be free, convenient though the hammer was, inviting though his speckled crown might be.

So, a year later, I was back where I started. But it was nice to start all over again. There was still hope, anyhow. Maybe this time I'd get it right. I thought I knew what 'it' was. It was out there somewhere; I'd know it when I happened onto it. The dream adjusts, but not the dreaming.

Mrs Luby's helped. I had a whole summer to settle in there by myself: Eamon had to go to England to earn his keep for the year. But I felt not at all lonesome. I was well-fed. I could stroll over to Peg's whenever I wanted to watch television, could even stay up late with her to watch *That Was The Week That Was*, which, like Profumo (the two seemed to blur), I couldn't quite fathom the ins and outs of: but everyone else was laughing and saying how marvellous, so I did too. The Stella was nearby, and other cinemas only up the road a bit – the Kenilworth, the Classic, Terenure . . . . Mrs Luby had a little padlock on the 'phone, but I was hardly likely to be telephoning anybody. Apart from the regularity with which sardines on toast were served, I had no complaints. It was a strange time.

And I read. Unconsciously suspicious of sitting so prettily, perhaps, it struck me that the nicest way to spend the summer would be to sit by the Valor in the guests' living-room and gorge myself on books' articulate, redemptive silences.

Reading was the most comprehensive and, it seems, most natural expression I could manage that I was living my own life. Nobody for tennis. The one club I might have joined was the Film Society, but that I thought to be off-limits. Dances were too dear. But there was a library to love: that red-brick pileen on the corner of Leinster Road was my Vatican, my Mecca, a Croke Park of the intellect, a veritable Dublin. There was also one of the Banba Books chain nearby on the opposite side, specializing in kids' novelties and second-hand paperbacks; among the latter it was possible to find some of the banned (was the name of the place a complicated pun!) – I found *Catch-22* there; also just about the only 'Irish' book besides *Borstal Boy* I read at that time, *The Ginger Man*. I didn't care for the Irish writing that Mr Dangerfield represented, it was too loose and free; besides, I was developing a nasty little prejudice against students. As for Behan – much as I enjoyed *Borstal Boy*, the man himself struck me as Sebastian in the flesh. Clean writing for the mind alone was what I desired, not laughs for the belly.

I might have found what I was looking for in other Irish writers of the day, some of whose names I'd heard. But nobody ever talked about them. I hardly ever found their books in paperback, more evidence that they weren't famous or properly modern, and so I didn't bother looking for them in the library. Camus also – later such a pebble on a dry tongue – proved elusive. Okay: Meursault shot the fella on the beach, fair enough; but then I thought there was going to be blood and murder altogether – shoot-out at the Oran corral. But no. It was too unlike a movie for me to feel at ease with it. Somerset Maugham was much more like it: *The Moon and Sixpence*, *The Razor's Edge* were great – colour applied with a sweeping-brush, problems introduced with all the chilling drama of venomous inoculations: that's the style, thought I. The trouble with Maugham, though, was that all his characters wore suits. So when Woodfall Films (I had Da's habit of noticing names) began being popular and *The Loneliness of the Long Distance Runner* came out, it was a wonderfully pleasant shock; now – *this* really is the style, I thought. That lad was a real borstal boy, and ever would be, and he didn't care. I was jealous. Why couldn't I be a sonovabitch too? I concluded that this failure came from not being English.

Eamon came back and we chummed up. We went to the Stella for the worn forties' thrillers they invariably had on Sunday nights. We went for walks whenever he began to overload with bookwork, and he was an Ardnacrusha at the books. I admired him. I feared his steely diligence. His discipline, his fussy phalanx of lapel-pocket biros, his strict budgeting of time and pleasure, his girllessness, his somewhat elderly intensity of purpose made me glad I was not at Earlsfort Terrace after all, particularly now that things were going more agreeably at Kevin Street. It was strange: here was Eamon reading and calculating Irish stuff for all he was worth, and all – as he cynically conceded – in order to land a half-way decent job in Canada or South Africa, whereas I, with little or no effort, learning English stuff, was probably going to stay at home. And all the time he remained a model citizen: he neither smoked nor drank and sent a parcel of soiled clothes home weekly to his mother.

But he didn't live by bread and Mrs Luby's fries alone. Every Saturday lunchtime he went to the Universal, Wicklow Street, for a taste of sophistication. Chinese. His regular lunch partner was a B.Ag. in the making, a quiet type from Elphin called Willy; but a time or two – when Franz took a Saturday off, sometimes Peg let me go at half-twelve instead of quarter to one – I joined them for number twelve (the curried brimstone) or the Egg Too Long (number five). 'It fills you up'; it was only years later I found out that meant it wasn't a Chinese meal. You had to be early to get a table. In general, I think Eamon was relieved when I didn't turn up. He liked to keep his home life distinct from such student activities as he participated in, and didn't want to be sitting next to the only person in the room not wearing a college scarf. I'd lived long enough with Mam to accept that he was entirely justified in his attitude. I, a Tech boy, was naturally on a lower level to him, and I was glad that I now recognized and identified with that level, and was grateful for its reduced seriousness and self-denial.

But I did still feel the pangs of the original dream when Eamon went on about the L & H. Early in my walks down Hatch Street to Radionics, I'd slink crestfallen past UCD. But I'd cured myself, I thought, by telling myself they were all snobs there, all suits and ties, all aspirants to the boss class.

Now I heard they had this literary and historical thing, a kind of higher Hallowe'en party, and before lights out, too, at which perhaps I might meet a Callan Dunya, an Abbeyfeale Razumikhin, with the hope of finding something to yield to, as Roquentin did salvifically to Bessie Smith. 'Very witty fellas', he'd say in a considered manner, from the depths of a maturity unwontedly roused to enthusiasm. 'Brilliant; absolutely brilliant'; and I chafed at their namelessness, facelessness, fantasizing painfully, but only momentarily, about *semblables* and *frères*. 'You'd love it.' But when I said he ought to let me tag along, smuggle me in – didn't I look the part? ('I have longer hair than you!') it was always, 'Ah I can't. They'd catch me.'

Yet, to keep my spirits up, there was Eamon's vivid giggle, his incurious tolerance of Dublin, the willingness to suspend himself for a couple of hours before the Stella's Sunday night at the B-movies. We had the bond, too, of being together the evening Kennedy was shot. Mrs Luby stuck a head full of suds around the living-room door with the first word of it. We walked into town, hung around Earlsfort Terrace for a while (Eamon would neither let me go into college with him nor leave me outside, though by now we were limp with want of news), looked at one another vacantly, vacantly regarded the stunned faces on the bus returning to Rathmines, stood at the corner, watched without seeing what we could only consider the idiocy of life as it went on its way. That brumous November sky . . . . Our uncrowned king; the fell gang of renegade Catholic, Cuban, Castroite, Commies . . . . By jasus, I'd castro his fidel for him, quick and lively, so I would. Oh, my dark Jacqueline! That evening we didn't know how or what to think, or for weeks afterwards. Prayer was urged. It was the first time it seemed crucial to have a TV set.

By this time, too, however, I had a Tech pal, Mayo Eddie, who worked in the Soil Mechanics' lab at Trinity, and who was paired with me to weigh again in water and once more in air so that I could tell my fluent scientific lies. Our rendezvous was the Theatre de Luxe, Camden Street, which had a nice wide screen, small crowds and severe-looking girls with beehive hairdos who went throughout the auditorium spraying while the ads were on. The wide screen meant all the big pictures came there – *The Longest Day, The Guns of Navarone*; 89

the bigger the bang the brighter the billing. Dazed by the spectacle, we would ride the 12 home, hardly talking, feeling that the challenge to have a night out had been met with honour and that such pictures were as good as six pints or a French kiss at inducing the sensory deprivation without which a night out could be considered out.

One evening, Eddie surprised me by asking did I ever go to Croke Park? I did indeed, though more for old times' sake, or to see Mick O'Connell, than because I still thought myself a Gael. It wasn't for himself Eddie wanted to go, however, but for this 'wan' at work, a Miss Kelly of Clontarf, who was always onto him about going: apparently nobody at home would be seen dead in the place - 'she's a Protestant,' said Eddie. But off we went anyway, so eager – though we didn't dare admit it – that we were in time for the minor game. Galway and some other crowd played in the big match, Galway with some of their great team of Purcell and Stockwell and Jack Mahon still going strong. What I remember above all, though, was that on the way out, squeezing through the narrow gateways behind Hill 16, I ventured to put a hand around the waist of Miss Clontarf Kelly, protective, like. She squirmed around and gave me a smile that produced instant liquefaction of the knees. All day long she'd been good cousinly gas. She paid her way, but from embarrassment we insisted on buying her an orange. She roared at the game when we roared. I don't recall if she sang the national anthem – being so at ease with her by then, I didn't notice, but I wouldn't put it past her. And she was just the right height, a head shorter than me. I remember plumpness and a clear complexion. Was she wearing a floppy hat? Did she have curls? I remember softness of softness. A girl of a sunny day
. . . .

I never saw her again. This was not the plan at the time, though: at the time I was full of plans for this latest version of a lovely time forever. Confidently I squired herself and Eddie through the streets of houses that might have been transplanted direct from Church Lane, Lismore, and out at Newcomen Bridge, a way Da used to take me in years gone by. There Miss Kelly was put on a bus for home – oh, an ardent swain was I! But I thought it more important to act the
90 gentleman. It'd be fatal if she mistook me for a pushy culchie

– hence guidance by the waist, not the peremptory *hoult* of the hardened cattleman. Besides, didn't we have the rest of our lives?

I talked about her all the way back to tea, undeterred by Eddie's grunts and his, 'Well, it was a great game, anyhow.' He became more lively when I asked him for her work number: 'Oh cripes, don't ring her at all; they're fierce down on personal calls.' So I wrote down my number and told him to give it to her. 'Be sure, now.' 'Oh I will, yeah,' Eddie said, phlegmatically. But, of course, 'I forgot.' Then the next week she had the 'flu. 'Aw jay,' I said; and I couldn't afford grapes (never thinking I hadn't a clue what her address was). The following week she was off as well: 'I think I heard them saying her grandmother is after dying,' said Eddie, poker-faced. And muggins me swallowed this one too. *Shit*, I thought; she'll be in mourning now . . . . But maybe Protestants didn't mourn: hooray! . . .

It was another couple of weeks, and I was strongly thinking of starting a vigil in Lincoln Place in order to get another sight of her, when Eddie let me in on the open secret that I never in a million years would have suspected. 'Well, fuck you!' I said. How dare he not take my dreams to heart! 'You lousy fucker.' Strange as it seems now, telling Eddie exactly what I thought of him, and then stalking off, felt at the time at least as important as Miss Clontarf bliss.

It was in the spring after Franz's operation and Brendan Behan's funeral. April, a fine day: that's how I remember the bolt from the blue.

All had been right with the world. Kevin Street was turning out to be a summer stroll. We had a nice teacher for the electricity classes, Mr Sloan, who worked at Pye, I think, and who had a nice, soft Northern accent. Physics was the same physics as ever, and I heard by way of Peg, who had heard from the teacher's mother, a client, that I was doing fine. I'd even worked out a way to fake parallax. My confidence was growing (I was beginning to see how I had never allowed it space and time enough in which to make its necessary adjustments). I won't pretend that Mr Sloan jumped out of his suit when I, alone of all the class, was able to explain how transistors worked on the basis of theory already acquired, but he did remark, in quiet surprise, 'vair' guid'; oh, and didn't I beam!

Work, too, had been less burdensome of late. That was because Franz had been taken bad and had spent at least a fortnight in hospital (God's door act once more creating revolutionary justice). We mice had thrived indeed, or at least one had. And Franz's return did not immediately overshadow my good mood. He'd had a blood transfusion, and told everyone who crossed his path that he was an Irishman; oh yes, he had Irish blood in him. Yet not even the fiftieth repetition of what I normally would have considered a monstrous lie and slander – and a lousy joke, which was worse – inclined me to reach for the hammer. I was relaxed. That was the trouble.

We were having the ten o'clock scone and cuppa. Talk was desultory. I suppose Peg and Franz may have been going over what news the newspapers had while he was sick, not that Franz showed much interest in the play of man and events; they probably were doing nothing more (nothing less) than renewing the sound of their voices for each other – a pre-electronic hearing test – with news as pretext. However it was, the name of Brendan Behan came up, the size of the funeral, the amount of his will. Out of nowhere I heard Franz say: 'Ja, he was a disgrace to his country'. And out of a different nowhere I heard myself instantaneously inquire, half-shouting: 'What about you?'

Twenty years later, I still hardly know what I meant, except that I meant it as Peg and Franz immediately understood it, a xenophobic slur, a chunk from the hand that fed me. I suppose I meant that, blood transfusions notwithstanding, I thought he had no right to criticize Behan – Franz, a man who probably didn't even know where Sundrive Road was. Yet it also seems – and this is what puzzles me – that I considered Franz a disgrace to his country. Why should I think that? What exactly did I mean by it? Did I imagine him a blackmarketeer, or consci? Did I picture him sipping his chicory roast or acorn extract as he drank in the latest *Het Vlammsche Land*? Did I see him on the platform at Malines? – hardly. Or with the Rexists? Or hearing mass with that devout Catholic, Gueleiter Degrelle?

I don't know. I only knew that now the word was out. This time it was pride I'd singed, not bakelite. Silence descended.

We walked around for days as though our heads were stuck in buckets. And finally, too, it seemed, Peg gave up. She didn't approach me with suggestions about making up. She made no effort to bring together sulky victim and stunned aggressor. I caught her eye a time or two but all I saw in it was an annoyed look, saying, 'Bloody fool!' I'd blown all the circuits. The clone, through no will of his own, had refused to be born. After a couple of days, Franz said, not looking at me, 'I want some notice, you know'. So he wants me to be the one to leave, I thought: well, that was tolerant of him . . . Peg must have . . . . 'Okay,' I said, 'I'm giving you a fortnight's notice'. Steam flew from Franz's ears, and the windows rattled. 'And I give you wahn whik!' he screamed.

4

The big job of the day came first thing – leaving Mrs Luby as though everything was the same as ever. I whistled, I hummed; out I bustled, business-like. Deception seemed the better part of valour because I imagined that somebody of my landlady's age would consider sacking a shameful eventuality; I had already heard a woman of roughly her age – Mam – appraise it as moral delinquency of a particularly culpable nature on the part of the sackee. Also, there was the question of rent. I had some holiday money – the final pay-off was punctilious – so was set for a couple of weeks. But from Eamon's absence the previous summer, not to mention long conversations over motherly cups of tea about Vincent and Brendan and Finbar and other predecessors – their peccadilloes, their careers, the speed with which they had discharged themselves from her tightly-run ship – I was fully aware of the stock Mrs Luby put on continuity of tenure. And since she seemed pleased with me – or at least she had made a point of telling me I was clean – I knew she expected a lot of me; two or three years at least, if not more – I was young, not a student, not a drinker, not a phoner, not a bit of trouble: oh, I was a   93 landlady's delight (not alive).

In all other respects, however, my high spirits in the early morning were not fake. 'The bullet', 'the boot', which I had received seemed merely to have elevated me into a pleasant and lofty trajectory, all the more pleasant since there was no landfall immediately in sight. My cards were a passport to an undiscovered, yet surely very pleasant country. So I thought, sauntering down to Belgrave Square for a 12 to town – very handy, that 12 (I was upstairs; the day's first Gold Leaf was doing a grand, insidious job of mollifying the aftertaste of black pudding and red tea): it brought me through the good parts of the life I'd lately left – past the Bleeding Horse, and Cavey's, past MacDonald's, the newsagent near the corner of Pleasant Street – without letting me see the site of my confinement, as I very promptly thought it. I even thought of older days, except that I was now taking myself by the hand to do the town. I was even one of the Unemployed, and (I understood them now, I thought) I felt no fear at all. I could lie down in the middle of O'Connell Bridge, if I really wanted to: who was to stop me?

For perhaps my first three days of furlough, I wallowed. I walked the quays. How pleasant to linger by the book-troughs outside Webb's and its cousin on Bachelor's Walk, opposite, The Dublin Bookshop. How charming to wander dusty back-streets at dusty hours, half-two on a Wednesday afternoon; a quarter to eleven on Tuesdays. I tended to avoid thoroughfares. I'd seen them before. (I wasn't able to afford them.) The city became a place of short-cuts and laneways, the sites of jute warehouses and idle loading docks, places suspended in the long moment between the dying echo of the last harness-clink and hoof-clop and the incipient rumble of the juggernaut truck. Empty bays, mild mote-filled air . . . .

Poor places. I began to see this, for the first time. Because I was on foot I saw a Dublin new to me. The oul-lads sitting in the little park near Saint Patrick's and Iveagh House struck me as less lucky, now that I could see their caved-in faces and their addled body language, instead of passing them on the Sundrive bus and envying them for being Dubliners. The urchins scampering in the black hallways of Sean MacDermott Street and Summerhill were not superior versions of the shoeless gamins, my playmates in Church Lane. Instead, I

94

found, they were foreign and frightening in their raucous intensity. I saw them, in their quickness and knowledge of the streets, as capable of committing crime, just as I'd heard grown-ups continually allege of them. I realized they lived where there were crimes to commit. They weren't picturesque at all, suddenly. I seemed to see their futurelessness: I began to be afraid. I'd heard that Sean MacDermott Street was where whores lived. I dreamt I was approached by one, a hefty piece, tight-fitting dress of shocking pink, strange feathery accessories. A ludicrous conversation ensued, me pleading poverty, she smirkingly identifying herself as the charity that begins at home. Uncannily bright, daylit streets, and a twisting, turning, rapid forced march through them. Then I vertiginously plummet down a hallway black as sin . . . I thought I had discovered why city people walk quickly, and with a style of quickness. I began to walk quickly, but that only revealed to me the sooner that I didn't know where I was going, that I had nowhere to go.

And on the other side of town, in the purlieu of the Castle, I also started seeing things I'd never seen before. This was Dublin's old raddled body, stripped of the dressed-stone façades, grey, withering places belying their colourful names – Winetavern Street; The Liberties. Streets not broad, but narrow. Images from schoolbooks: Silken Thomas's head on a spike, Lord Edward weltering in his blood, Emmet swinging while their ladyships looked on. Gore and failure; crumbling laneways and sunless precincts. It would be better not to have to look at this, the meeting of a non-future with a past that clanked its chains around places that seemed made of frozen dust. It would be better had I bitten my tongue and stayed in Harcourt Street, which at least I knew. I walked down Francis Street and foresaw a history of poverty for myself. In Meath Street I thought I'd surely go to the dogs. Rain was a problem: my cardboard shoes of elegant cut began to leak. I was afraid to face Mrs Luby with a drowned-rat look. I wondered how the sandwich-board men got their interesting, airy positions; what patronage provided the parking attendants with their appointments, which I knew had to be official since they wore caps. Sheltering under a Dame Street awning, I gazed with envy at the man propping (being propped by) a bespectacled sign pointing towards the opticians in Fownes Street.

I suppose I should have prayed. When I was small, I'd once asked Chrissy what would I be, prompted perhaps by Doris Day's 'Que sera, sera', though obviously expecting a more definitive response than the frankly pagan doctrine espoused in that chartbuster's chorus. Wise Chrissy said to pray: Holy God would tell me. I pressed her, but she was firm. Yes, He'd told Uncle Frankie to be an engineer and Aunt Kathleen to be a scientist. 'And what did He tell you to do?' I persisted. 'He told me I'd be at home looking after me mother,' Chrissy said. That settled it. But she didn't stay, she went away. She and Da – my two great loves – had gone and made out lives for themselves, and didn't seem to give a damn if that was sin or not.

Yet, it did not occur to me that with those two life-supports cut off I now was left with God. For one thing, I found His presence much less persuasive in the city. Now that I was paying rent, the Church's spiritual landlordism lost its appeal. Twelve mass in the green-domed hanger of Rathmines parish church was largely a yawn. There was no hurling club news. The charity of our prayers was requested for the repose of the souls of total strangers. There was the customary fashion show, of course: but what it gained in novelty and sophistication over its counterpart at second mass in Lismore was offset by the girls remaining unknown and placeless – and anyhow, the twelve was always packed, so I never could get a proper eyeful. Confession was like going to the post office. 'Bless me Father for I have two letters, three postcards and a registered package.' The items were franked, the toll exacted: 'Okay, two decades of the Joyful Mysteries – thank you – Next!' But then, I wasn't alive enough to make confession interesting.

I began to question what else I had going for me, religiously speaking. Not a whole lot, it seemed. I never had much time for the various prostrations and time-surrendering supplications – novenas, First Fridays, sodalities, confraternities – identification with which secured one an address on the *via dolorosa* which, by all accounts, life was. I did not cultivate devotion to recommended patrons and intermediaries. If I was interested in saints at all it was in the marginal lads: St Swithin the rainmaker, St Joseph of Cupertino (a sovereign at exam time), or St Vitus the twitcher. The best thing I'd discovered in old Dublin was a church to St Audoen, whom I identified immediately as the patron of cinema chains.

It began to dawn on me that my religion was my culture, not a relationship with a deity. And when I found that culture's institution, the Church, seemed banal and unilluminating – as grey and friable and redolent of denial as the walls of ancient history – then I didn't know exactly what was left. I didn't think I could meet man-to-man with God; that was what Protestants thought themselves good enough to do. And I knew I wasn't one of them. So what was I? And where was I, who sidled past St Michan's on the other side: And what to do, now that prayer, the only form of serious thinking I'd ever come across, no longer seemed the very thing?

It must have been raining, and I must have been on my way to Hanna's, Nassau Street. Otherwise I don't know what would have brought me to Creation Arcade, Brown Thomas's and such snootiness. Even the accident of weather, however, does not explain why I went into that place of silks and unguents, much less why, once there, I went to see if the Little Theatre was still in it. I remembered from the old days that Da sometimes would march us through a show of paintings or photos in the Little Theatre, his ten-minute reward for dawdling through the store people, aisles spiced with fabrics in jade and sandalwood which Mam fondled absently, tweed suits which she inspected with an ex-seamstress's hawkish eye, dreaming perhaps of what a Sybil Connolly was lost in her. (Mam dreaming. Mam on holiday: Mam young, years condense, years expand . . . .)

Whether or not the old days were guiding me, here I was, and sure enough some low-voiced, well-heeled types were in the theatre doorway. An easel with a sign announced a show of some kind – I hardly took it in before I entered, thinking that least it would let my poor shoes relax. There were some photos on the wall, but much more unexpectedly on tables underneath them were machines. I didn't know what kind they were but they looked as if they were on speaking tems with electricity because they had knobs and dials and were dressed in the shiny plastic of new technology. I didn't recognize any of their names – Lumière, Kindermann – but at least they were bigger than hearing aids, and therefore – for all their exhibition-abject, Sunday-suited shyness – struck me as a vaguely positive step in some direction or other.

A man approached. He looked young – his brown eyes glistened; his somewhat swarthy face was unlined. He asked if he could help me. His tone was outgoing, interested, nothing like the icy discriminating way that shop-help had been lately asking me the same thing. I invited him to explain the yokes. And behold, they were electric! One was a photo-copier, the other a dry mounter – whatever that was, but it didn't matter: at the sight of something new the world enlarged for me again. The streets grew broad, the Bovril sign lit up. So when the man's spiel was done, I heard myself say, as bold as brass (emboldened both by novelty and my brasslessness), 'Well, I suppose you'll be looking for a good man to service these?' The man cocked his head at me, whether in suppressed laughter or genuine appraisal I wasn't able to make out. But then he said, 'I might, if I sell any'; and I knew he was a good sort; it wasn't often I came across such candour – even youngish men like him were often apparently unable to afford it. Again made bold, I matched his directness with my own: 'Well, I'm your man!' said I.

This time he might well have smiled, but I was too busy telling him about my excellent qualifications, my years of experience, my Kevin-Street sojourn (did he know I got first in the class in the Christmas test?); no doubt about it, he'd be doing himself a favour by letting someone like me into the business. 'Well, actually,' he said, 'the main business is photo-finishing'. But this was great as well, as I gave him to understand by mentioning that my father was a member of the Irish Film Society. 'Well, we'll see,' the man said, and gave me his hand. 'My name is Ken. I'll be in touch. And when I wrote my address down for him: 'That's very near us; we're in Upper Rathmines Road'. There, see! That was definitely a sign; somebody up there likes me after all; God looks after his lodgers.

I don't know what I did then. If it had been raining I'd have sung in it, and swung from the lamp-posts too; if dry, my every follicle and nerve-end must just have gone *doo-dee-doo-doo* to themselves. What an extremely nice man; what a most interesting and enjoyable conversation! And those machines were clearly the cat's pajamas, obviously the last word – in what, though? Ken had explained, but of course I wasn't able to remember. One thing copied photos, didn't it, and wasn't the other a kind of oven in which the mounting of your photos could be finished dryly? It looked like a little oven. Or possibly a TV set. Well, anyway; sure I'd pick it up as I went along. What mattered at the moment was that a man had spoken to me, a stranger.

At this remove, of course, I see that I must have struck Ken less as Beau Soudreur, technician *extraordinaire*, than as an ill-kempt youngster, who still hadn't managed gash-free shaving, whose Siemens razor had gone the way of all his machines from the Hornby clockwork train onwards (not to mention all the machines unlucky enough to make his acquaintance); someone for whom interviews took place on the radio – not in real life; someone to whom the term 'application form' had no meaning; a fooleen who believed that 'I'll be in touch' could only be meant insincerely in a movie. And yet he'd spoken.

And of course I knew I'd have a letter from him. Probably before the year was out I'd have a little van, like the green-and-white RenTel vans that some of my ex-classmates from Kevin Street drove; except from now on they would be the jealous ones. Those oven things would sell like hotcakes in Foxrock and Greystones, where, I imagined, there were women with all the time in the world for such figaries. 'Will I hook it up for you, missus? (heh-heh-heh). Where would you like it?' Surely it wasn't too much to ask that one of these fine, isolated ladies with sensibly small families off in school, and little left to do but wait for *Mrs Dale's Diary* to come on, would catch my drift?

In the New Year, then (all out of ovens after the Christmas rush), I'd probably be promoted to camera-work – someone had to make the photos so they could be finished, hadn't they? I remembered Da proudly sporting his Agfa Isolette on summer holiday in Lismore, posing me at the miniature beach called the Bark Yard made by the Owbeg running low. 'F16 at a 20th,' he'd mutter, worrisomely, staring into the delicate rainbow and strange bat's-wing fabric that somehow made the whole thing work. He used to let me do the winding on. So I knew my way around a camera, right enough . . . . Soon I'd be able to show that Da of mine a thing or two. Then he'd be proud. Then he would recognize in me a coming man, and I'd at last know who I was. And this time no mistakes. This time the instantaneity and minutiae of work would be mine to 99 command. This time, I swore, the appropriate chemistry would definitely, once and for all, coax forth an agreeable image.

Still, when the letter came, I had to read it a couple of times before properly taking it in. All it said was that Ken had decided to take me on, would I start on so-and-so date, but to me my first business letter, the first envelope that mistered me in type, had more poetry in it than even 'The Destruction of Sennacherib' (a favourite since first I'd looked into it in second-year, because the Assyrians had cohorts who 'were gleaming in purple and gold', the Wexford colours). I had, it seemed, done something all by myself. And I was going to get six quid a week for it, too. Damn decent of Ken, that. It didn't surprise me one bit to learn a little later that he was a Protestant. I'd always heard at home what decent types they were when it came to money matters. And when, that June Monday, I turned up at Findlater's in Rathmines – we worked in rooms above the shop – and climbed the stairs and caught the tang of onions and tomatoes and bananas and thought of Dowd's, the fruit distributors in Lismore, Protestants too, but true-blue Fianna Fáils, givers of steady work to the town, providers of lifts to Dublin in their trucks, or to friends of Tony, my contemporary, to the seaside at Clonea or Stradbally in their Nash Rambler with the horn that was a rim inside the steering-wheel, I knew then that happy days were here again and that once more I could be comfortably at home with strangers.

There was Anne, Frances, Margaret, June and Chris, all girls except Anne, who was a woman: she swore at things and people when they didn't work and smoked Churchman No. 1, which even then were not sold everywhere, a strong, fat smoke, mannishly untipped. For any woman to light up one of those – and Anne's Ronson was well cared for; it had hair-trigger ignition – was a fifteen-minute exhibition of hard neck and brazen cheek. In Lismore she would have been known as a strap, if not a virago, and I was half-afraid of her in case I forgot myself when she had cause to shout at me and landed one of those soubriquets on her. I need not have feared. After watching me closely the first morning when, with that technical aplomb which was mine alone to command and deploy, I

caused greenish smoke to ooze sadly and unstoppably out of

a Lumière, Anne sighed expresively and thereafter held her
peace.

Which was fine, because the other girls were grand gas. I got
on with them so easily that I didn't even care that they looked
more like people's sisters than they did dames: one or two of
them may conceivably have been sufficiently sisterly to have
spots, enabling me to see them as no better off than me and
myself as no worse off than them, for which relief much
thanks. They were all Protestants, as well, and Chris, as
though to define the delightful strangeness of it all, was
English, the first person I had met who had come from there to
Ireland to work.

They all helped relieve the aftershocks of my mornings'
disasters when we trooped off for elevenses to that fair-sized
room, fronted by plastic fascia and all formica inside, near the
Cecil Fine on Rathmines Road. Not that the coffee itself was
not a diversion. It was made to a home recipe whose main
ingredients seemed to be nutmeg, Horlicks and Scott's
Emulsion, all estimable items in their own right (who, of my
generation, dare cast a stone at Horlicks, sponsors – on
Luxembourg, no less – of Dan Dare, Pilot of the Future), but in
combination . . . . As far as I could make out, this blend was
deliberately interfered with by scorched milk, American
unseemliness which took place inside a latter-day descendant
of the iron horse, a sort of aluminium pony, through whose
nether orifices the fluid eventually seeped, gasping and
frothing. A not-young-man with thinning hair and wizening
phizzog placed the cups on the counter for us, wordlessly
accepting our shilling pieces in exchange. It beat all. Previously, coffee was something a woman – a waitress or a relative
– would provide; it usually went in my mind along with treats
and I'd assumed its existence depended on boiling water.
Come home, Irel; all is forgiven! Later I regretted that I hadn't
paid more attention to the place: it must have been
somewhere like it that Tommy Steele was discovered.

Of course I had no idea then that there soon would come a
time when I'd find things English coming in handy. England
had been a dark cloud east of the Customs House during my
ten-day walkabout, admittedly. But those days were gone;
from now on, nothing but blue skies and plain sailing. Ken's
business mainly was colour processing: I felt the metaphorical

possibilities of a career in it – every man his own Bovril sign. Colour was being discovered wholesale – in people, in ads. Colour was a rhetoric of unsameness and of possibility. *A White Sportscoat and a Pink Carnation.* Another novelty with which I could immediately identify. *Cherry Pink and Apple-Blossom White* – cha-cha-cha! I *was* starting over. Breaking for coffee, lunching sensibly on meat and two veg in the crammed parlour above Ferguson's cake-shop, lounging by the sinks in the back room waiting for the photos to finish themselves, all I felt was acceptance and relief.

I was a boy. I didn't kiss the girls, so I had a chance to make them laugh. Ken himself contributed to the boyish mood. 'Hell's bells and buckets of blood!' he'd exclaim. 'Jolly hockey sticks.' He had a thousand ways of saying splendid. He lunched with us. He went to the coffee-bar with us, and sometimes stood a round, even rising to a Jacob's Club if anyone wanted one. Knowing I lived near, he'd ask me to stay an extra hour an odd evening and afterwards he'd buy me chop and chips at Dinky Snacks, opposite the start of Leinster Road, and talk about his plans, ask me what I thought: his myriad plans, and how he seemed to effervesce with love for every one of them. I'd never come across a superior as open and as lively, had never seen work considered a pleasure not a burden, had never thought to find outside of books and banners equality and fraternity. Here, I thought, was someone to be like at last, someone obviously at liberty to believe in his own energy, for whom the world as he found it was right enough. My own version of that liberty – that's what I need.

Work, alas, did not provide it. Improvement in pay, atmosphere and conditions did not mean that I was less good-for-nothing now than I had ever been. Once more, machines, as soon as I had responsibility for them, ceased to be instruments of wonder and futurity and became agents of repressive tedious fact. Aesthetic distance disappeared; the essential, impenetrable difference of things rose up to pull me by the nose and boot me on the behind. It was as though my conscience wouldn't let me get things right, as if to snick the shutter freely or remove the lens cap, not to mention the whole presumptuous process of converting thing to image (the image becoming, as a result, a thing in itself as well as a substitute for the real thing, which in turn seemed to possess a

merely inept, potentially obsolescent reality) – all this instinc-
tively seemed to me to imply identification with the sin of
pride, puny pride, Adam's pathetic self-rehabilitation . . . .
How could I, my own mind inchoate and unratified, presume
to know the mind of an it? Little me: no confidence in the
confidence trick of making do, no confidence to do the trick,
and tricked by lack of confidence . . . .

Ken saw all this, or at least as much of it as he needed to, and
cut his losses. I became the boy. This was fun when we tooled
about in Ken's Rover 90 with walnut and leather inside, like a
parish priest's parlour. Ken was still a photographer; I carried
the Balcar flash through Jury's and the Hammond Lane
Foundry, pitched the special dove-grey umbrellas, checked
the connections like authentic Electrical Man (in case anyone
was watching). But such jaunts were few, and I was surprised
to find how little I got from them, once the novelty of the car
wore off, compared with the more difficult and, as I vaguely
thought, less fashionable Cabra trips with Franz. Most of the
time, the carrying I did was of rolls of film up and down the
Rathmines Road from the Kodak trade counter near Portobello
– a real messenger-boy, balancing long boxes on my shoulder,
labouring by the chapel without saluting it, past the Swastika
Laundry, and the tall, blank-looking houses that seemed to
have no roofs, their doorjambs peppered with white bell-
presses, all belonging to people more interesting than I,
members of the Monaghanmen's Association, past pupils of
St Jarlath's or some other school that had won something,
done something, denoted a prominent diocese or a strange-
sounding place (oh for affiliation with St Nathy's,
Ballaghaderreen . . . .). Here dwelt the sisters of inter-county
hurlers, people with the right connections due to their
exposure at an early age to networking Muintir na Tíre-style.
Hearth-warmer of the year, Horseleap branch, Irish
Countrywomen's Association. Knitter of the month:
crocheteuse of the half-century. My mouth watered at the
thought of their barm brack. I'd hail their brothers heartily as
they came throbbing through the haggard on th'oul Fordson
Major. I thought of them and lost track of my counting in the
darkroom (we developed reels by hand, the creels of them had
to be agitated, lifted and drained in each of the three solutions
every so often: say *a thousand and one*, that's a second . . .). 103

Now that I was the boy I'd fantasized about in Harcourt Street, I once more wanted something else, pined for difference all over again – would nothing ever change me? Was there some devil in me making me impervious to the present? How about scones with raisins in them, plump and moist as a frog's belly, and to follow, Madeira cake the yellow of May sunshine: tea at four on Sunday, served on a lace tablecloth her sister the nun made . . . ?

So there seemed nothing for it but to leave Mrs Luby for life, liberty and the pursuit of happiness in bedsitterland, the other that is the eternal future seducing me again: one more small leaving, what odds could it make among so many? I didn't realize, however, that I had got myself caught up in my first clear-cut autonomous decision, until, quite unexpectedly, I was called upon to defend it. Mrs L. somberly predicted ruin and starvation would instantly attend me in the wake of such a headstrong, foolhardy move: what was I thinking of at all, at all. She offered to do lunch for me. Alternatively, 'Well I can see you won't be said by someone who's only thinking of your own good' ('I know that, ma'am'); 'But I won't stand in your way. I only hope you won't regret it.' That moral sandbag, more substantial and more winning than a year of lunches. In the end, I told her some lie. The lie was in the service of a higher truth, of which I was persuaded: by resembling my culchie compatriots in domestic circumstances, I might meet some of them. I didn't dare say – to Mrs Luby, much less to myself – that I had no future with Ken, either; all I could do there now was watch for the time when he started letting me down less gently whenever I let him down. I couldn't bear the thought that perhaps the bedsit was the last resort. I just availed myself of the efficient machinery of moving – a trip one lunchtime to *The Evening Press* small ads. So it was official now: I'd enlisted in the columns of need . . . . Closing doors, opening others . . . . But I deflected those kind of thoughts as well.

The wording of the ad gave me a lot of trouble. I wanted mine to be among the first to catch the eye, but could come up with nothing alphabetically pre-eminent, deciding that 'A bastard about cleanliness' would probably not go down too well. I didn't know until I collected the replies to the box number how effectively banalities communicate. They came from Drumcondra, though I'd specified south side; a woman from Walkinstown wrote on baby-blue paper offering the room of a first child who would never arrive or who had lately died. And I was 'Dear Sir' to landladies across the city, ones with teeth and without, with whiskers and without, with schooling and barely able to sign their names. The palm of my three-pound weekly payment, however, I awarded to Mrs O'Connell of Leinster Road. In exchange I received the back room in her first floor. She retained the whole ground floor for herself, though I could hang my Bri-Nylon drip-dry shirts on her line if I liked (I'd have to get some): the flash of her porcelain dentures when she said that reminded me of the way the tabs with figures appeared on a cash register.

It was a dark room with a poor aspect. The wallpaper was brown on brown, November leaves at rest on mulch. It seemed welded to the wall, and had a sheen, possibly of the hair-oil of former tenants who'd banged their head against it. The large sink was the colour and consistency of the landlady's teeth; the bed had a hammock middle; a broken electric fire hid in the wardrobe, to save its blushes; the gas cooker looked like it saw action in the cockpit of Stephenson's rocket. 'An awful quiet fella (Leitrim I think he is),' lived on the second floor, Mrs O'Connell confided to me at the top of her voice. Awful invisible, too, he was. Some evenings there'd be a whiff of Brylcreem on the stairs, but that was as close as I came to the kind I was, in theory, seeking. He was off to a dance, probably.

The lady in the room next door to me was almost as invisible but more intriguing. Mrs Gamage was an unlined Englishwoman – still with a shy, girlish simper; still with a wardrobe of flounces, of a little lace at throat and wrists – who had spent her working life on stage all summer in Blackpool, Morecambe, Stockport, Douglas, Rhyl. 'She knew 'em all,' said Mrs O'Connell. 'Go on, tell him.' The ex-soubrette would simply smile and murmur, 'Happy days,' and continue staring out Mrs O's parlour window, waiting for her landlady to resume commentary on all the passing 'tramps'. For Mrs O'Connell spoke for everyone: she knew them all, seed, breed and generation, the cut of their gib and their gait of going. And if her English p.g. had retired her vocal chords, Mrs O. remained a veritable land of song, not to mention, when the kettle piped and the saucepans clashed, a warrior bard. Her 105 performances reached a weekly climacteric on Sunday mornings, when they prevented the house from sleeping past half-nine. Yet, she continually roared, God help her, she was to be pitied; and when that mood befell her, her vulpine face would stiffen and a faraway cast would come to her eye, as though tormented still by hurts from long ago, and she would screech her history out. They owned the finest hotel in either Nenagh or Bunclody, I can't remember. Her own man died in the rats of drink, 'the tramp'. And we were all tramps – to our faces, at that – Mrs Gamage no less than myself, no less than the lipstick-and-stiletto brigade from the square opposite: birds of passage, men of no furniture, concocters of midnight mixed grills, a desperate crowd entirely.

I sat on the bed, wondering .... At last the final strands of the umbilicus had been untidily hacked away. Who I was now rested in a stiff wardrobe drawer. A tramp .... Yes, well tramps went by themselves: the cap fit to that extent, the bed my own to lie on (cliché preserve me, *et nunc et semper*). But any tramps I'd seen seemed prone to having a bit of gas, and they always seemed to keep going. And, as the upstairs neighbour's scent reminded me, I was free to keep my own hours, to go out at bedtime and return with the milk, to go dancing even! (Do I have the confidence to be a solitary dance-goer? Well, it's about time to find out.) So maybe, after all, this – whatever it is – will be fine, when I get used to it. The best always must be yet: From downstairs, in a voice that sounded like tearing paper, I heard Mrs O. intone one of her reliables, 'Lonely, I wander the scenes of my childhood'. Not that, whatever else, I thought. Not that!

5

If Chris was in the darkroom, I'd be at the sink mixing up a vat of developer. If I was loading the reels for developing, she'd be finishing off the ektachrome plates outside. So, because we had the back room and the boring stuff to ourselves we got to talking: soon we were taking walks through Ranelagh where she had a room near the railway bridge, down Appian Way and Waterloo Road and back again along the vegetating, somnolent canal. Sundays on a bench along Mespil Road. Talking, talking. She too was just a boy at Ken's, the same as myself. Chris of Chingford. Walking out. Summer and shade on Wilton Terrace. Perhaps life could be simple after all. A slow waltz. What matter if I had rickets, I was in no hurry. Or so I thought whenever, without meaning to, we fell silent and unembarrassedly lingered on the passing moment, though very rarely did I savour moments for themselves: that seemed a recipe for anonymity, silence's synonym. I couldn't stay quiet: I was a broken lock, foaming and gushing.

At first it was, 'But enough of me, let's talk about you: do *you* think I need a haircut?' Chris – my God! – listened. I told her about Lismore, and school, and Monkstown and Harcourt Street, and as I spoke (as Chris tactfully clucked and t'ched and sighed appropriately) I began to hear again that I had a story of my own, a recitation of experiences which resembled none I'd ever heard, experiences which even seemed worth having since I could interest this tall, placid stranger in them, experiences which seemed almost tolerable because remembering them so clearly gave a kind of voyeuristic pleasure. I felt special again, through this naming of parts of myself. And not just by simply the naming, since I had done this off and on, vaguely and silently, when I thought I was reading *The Razor's Edge* or was effing and blinding Mrs O'Connell's interminable recitatives in the doric ('Flo-ho on laffly ri-vuhr'). It was naming to another that made the difference – better yet, an innocent other, who could neither contradict nor expropriate anything I said, but instead could only (made in England) politely accept it for whatever it was, unjudging. She was given to civil softly-spoken utterances of, 'Oh, dear'; to giggles similarly well-bred, not the fearsome secret satire of those wans in the Green and their screeching skitting. What a desperate bore I must have been! But I could not conceivably have thought myself one at the time. It wasn't long-suffering Chris I had in mind but the silence that at last I was scattering to the four winds, and the strange sense of reintegration that I felt, hearing myself being listened to.

Yet even when I was at my most stifling, Chris and I still usually managed to tread out a measure or two of common ground. Our ground was books. Did you read this? Have you read so-and-so? Chris taught me how to pronounce the phenomenon, the concept, Sartre, and solemn as a missioner, informed me that *The Age of Reason* was 'very important'. I replied that I had been living in it since I was seven, but the crack misfired and I felt obliged to cash in my intellectual's widow's mite by way of explanation, a rigmarole about what confession meant and how right could be told from wrong by seven. All news to Chris, who responded mildly: probably there were a lot of different explanations for things; she tried to keep an open mind, herself, personally . . . . Nothing daunted, I went: 'Pubs are about all you can keep open here, and you need a licence for that.' Wise, laughless Chris ignored me and went blithely on: 'Take Kafka, for example . . . . ' Another time she mentioned a certain Beckett, and communication breakdown. 'Silence is *so* important,' she declared. She was a real intellectual! My mouth hung open like a silly cow's. Evenings turned to dusk while we enthused. Dostoyevsky was the greatest. It was as if we had a Film Society for two.

Chris knew all about writers not just because she was a couple of years older than me and the beneficiary of an English education. The latter meant that she probably knew off by heart the servings of Bacon, Lamb and Hazlitt that we tried to digest – 'Of Simulation and Dissimulation'; spare us, O Lord – in the Leaving Cert. reader; on top of which, she'd passed through that pair of needle-eyes, the Eleven Plus and the O-levels, without a scratch to her hump. But that was not all. She was a writer herself, at present learning by what sounded an ideal method, a correspondence course. 'Cripes,' I exclaimed, 'that's powerful altogether,' thinking at once, in awed admiration, now there's a proper double life; look! – she's living her dreams and she's not a bit afraid . . . .

It was writing, 'in fact', said Chris that had brought her to Dublin. Here I had to laugh. Hadn't she heard that writers here were all dead? But Chris turned on me, ringingly affirming that the place was lousy with live ones. 'Where are they?' I demanded. 'Oh, pubs'; Chris waved a vague hand. 'Oh, chancers,' said I, surer in my denial than she in her rather more reasonable belief. 'One should travel, I think,' Chris said

108

mildly, then, as though in self-justification. 'Oh, absolutely!' I agreed, and spoke at length about my supposition that Dublin was as good a place as any to finish a course with the London School of Journalism. 'You make it sound like a slightly superior Grimsby,' said Chris, huffily. She herself saw it as the Petersburg or Prague of the British Isles, historical and grey, with a Haymarket (Moore Street) and desperate, homeless minds. No murders, I objected, wistfully recalling my Franz-and-hammer moments. But what really struck me in what she'd said was my attitude to Dublin. I was stunned. I had never for a minute suspected that Dublin might not be all I had imagined. Where had such a thought originated?

Whatever its origins, however, it led nowhere, the same as the inspiration about dances suggested by my neighbour, the invisible Leitrim-man. As I told Chris the next time we met, I had something else on my mind: 'Hey, y'know what I'm after thinking? I'm a writer, too!' My image of Chris has her replying at this point, 'Oh, you're a deep one,' politely coy: something like that. She may even have done so; I wasn't listening. I was too busy listing credentials. What I said was gospel truth. Didn't I get an Honour in English in the Leaving? Didn't I write the monologue which was the *sine qua non* and *pièce de résistance* of the Fifth Year Concert, the school's vale-diction to the Leaving Cert. class. The deathless opening lines came flooding back to bear me out: 'D-Day is the fifth of June / The days come quickly on / And Fifth Year now salutes the Sixth / Who next year will be gone.' (No wonder when it came to our turn, the following year, Jacko – Father O'Donnell, that is; that Fifth Year had to have it done for them – wrote, 'Lismore gave us Seoirse, composer of songs'!) And thanks to Chris I'd been brought back to this true – or, better, extremely enjoyable – version of myself. What was more, I told her, on my way to Kodak the other day I stepped in for a minute to Baggot's there at the corner of Castlewood Avenue – 'Don't tell Ken, sure you won't?' – and she'd never guess what I saw there: an Irish paperback (a Corkman called Mercier did it) by someone called Francis MacManus who was reported in the bio on the back to like helping young writers! Wouldn't this father-to-be be knocked sideways when he heard from me! 'Oh, you're writing something at the moment?' Chris eagerly enquired. With a fine show of reluctance, I eventually 109 conceded cagily that I was working on a little thing, crafting the lie like a born storyteller, availing myself at once of the new identity, the new start Chris had unwittingly midwifed. But what was I saying? I'd not put pen to paper. I tried to weasel out: 'The only trouble is, it'll have to be typed if I'm to send it in.' 'Let me do it,' said Chris. 'Great.' I said, curtly. Now I would have to write something, blast it.

The story, about four pages of typescript, was called 'Evening of the Star' and was a treatise on a louse/pop star whose surname was Glick ('Irish for clever', I explained to Chris, who, inexplicably, had thought he was meant to be Jewish), and who in his off-stage or, as I preferred to say in those days, 'real' life made a highly successful career as a biter of hands that never tired of feeding him. At this remove, it's the theme that leaps first and foremost to the guilty eye: at the time what was exciting was blackening all those pages, with never a thought that I seemed to be creating a character with just two distinguishing features, one that he lived in a glitzy fantasy land in which money was your only Bovril, the other that he possessed an ego and didn't care who knew it, two features as complementary, evidently, as evening and star.

Chris did an impeccable job of typing, and an even more remarkable one of keeping her opinions to herself. I bought an envelope at Baggot's and bore it with exaggerated vigilance, sitting inside on an 18, down the couple of hundred yards to her immaculate room in Ranelagh. It was a Sunday afternoon. The house was quiet. I remember how white the room seemed compared to mine: the acreage of lilies on her wallpaper, their cups voluptuous and wistful; Chris's scent of linen freshly pressed. 'Thanks a lot, Chris.' I placed my vesperal treasure in its pale postal sheath. Then – how I remember! – gorm and gormette stared at each other, suddenly expectant though as tentative as ever, and above all befuddled by the revelation that all our words had somehow managed not to utter what, unspeakably, was uppermost in our minds and which, as we both turned it down, deliberately, abashed, made future trysts perfunctory and intermittent, as we recognized, though from politeness never said, what a couple of painful cases we were.

Despite the eye-opening realization that it was not an evening of the star I needed but of some more corporeal entity, and that the appropriate place to apply for same was the Four Provinces or the Olympic, all energy remained directed at the pen which, as we'd learned in school, being mightier than the sword, was bound to be – here I was espousing a logic of things! – superior to the embarrassing (as we'd learned in school) mutton dagger. Now hopes rode high; I was full of plans again.

Even before Francis MacManus replied, I was already talking to Chris about the London School of Journalism, strangely enthusiastic now about further school, presumably because I was choosing this one. Since Chris had first mentioned the place I had indeed noticed its advertisement in the posh weeklies which on Saturday afternoons I leafed through in Eason's. It definitely seemed to be keeping proper company right enough, and I imagined that when the schoolers in journalism discovered what an exceptional student I was they'd open doors for me to *The Listener*, *John Bull*, *Time and Tide*, possibly with my picture cameo-style, like Mary Grant's used to be in *Woman's Own*. I had not only talent, memory reminded me (when memory's in the mood it can do anything, shape and reshape personality with the mercy that indefinitely connotes). I had tradition. Grandfather Royce had been associated with the Enniscorthy *Echo*. Aunt Chris had penned the 'Lismore Notes' for the Dungarvan *Observer*, once, for six weeks or so.

So off I wrote – trenchant and flowery; prolix and puerile – for full particulars, which eventually came back – weren't they wicked teasers not to be in as big a hurry as I expressly divulged to their good selves that their faithful servant (which I remained, needless to say) was! (It was the same years before, dealing with Philatelic services of Goole, Yorks, in order to build the biggest and best stamp album that tips from relations could buy: waiting for orders to be filled was like sitting through a Sunday sermon with a full bladder). The English seemed to be like that, not ones to make much of things. Take Chris, now, and my grand story – not a peep, really. 'Very interesting,' when we spoke later; sure couldn't she tell how little nourishment that was? The Chris of the white room and unsisterly melting mood I ruthlessly suppressed, concluding obscurely that non-intellectual camaraderie would be hypocritical, as, I believed, all bonds based on feeling were.

111

And then, when the letter did come, with all the intriguing paraphernalia, it turned out they wanted not my genius, but money! Oh, a two-faced crowd of tricksters, them English. I thanked my lucky stars that I had kept my wits about me while waiting for that London letter, and had been able to bethink myself, who I was and where I'd come from, head swelled, resembling bladder of yore, all due to my second mister letter, from F. MacManus. It was obvious from the word go that he would write, of course, not because, or not only because, of my stellar performance, but because I still lived in a world where things happened because I expected them to – not as many things as I wanted, perhaps; but still, enough to keep me nervous and unsettled, hence, as I thought, alive. Stone grey paper; Radio Éireann at its head. I stupidly hadn't thought of that when I wrote my covering note, but, of course, it struck me immediately now: a job *in radio* as a writer. He'd probably start me off small, something like 'This Week's Appeal', then after a month or two I'd be promoted to *The Foley Family* – Tom and Alice the gas newly weds: the Huggetts of Marino, the Burns and Allens of Bulfin Road. They were still on, of course (I had hardly heard a radio since leaving Monkstown), waiting for me to help them have the whole country doubled-up in stitches. This MacManus probably hadn't done his homework, didn't know my radio credentials went way back. But I'd be telling him.

As it happened, Radio Éireann chose not to pursue my services at that time. But the letter was sweetness itself. (Its unlikelihood makes it sweeter with each passing year.) I could be a writer, I was told, 'a lyrical writer, a satirical writer' (I quote, with ease, from memory), but I would have to write about what I knew, 'even if it's only a swim in the canal'. At which advice I expostulated with Chris. Maybe this fellow had written books and had a cushy job, but he didn't know the first thing about being a writer, because what being a writer means is writing about what you don't know, using the oul' imagination, living the secret, independent life of the mind within. Ideas. Murders. The Moon. The Sixpence. I knew so little I didn't even know what I knew. I didn't know – although I very well might have, given recent experiences – that it was not a matter of mind against the world. It was a lot more confusing and demoralizing than that: mind in the world.

I had the good grace not to communicate any of this to my well-disposed but all too temporary mentor. And I had the ill-grace not to thank him for his startling generosity, deciding that I would wait to write again until I had another slab of prose to impose upon those conscientious shoulders of his. So, we never met, and Chris was needlessly deprived of a chance to meet an Irish writer, about whom she might have written, earned a few bob, paid off a pressing instalment of the debt to her more sophisticated, much less personal, tutelage, gone on a skite (she often wanted me to go to a pub with her – she couldn't go alone – but I wouldn't: 'Pubs are for country mugs – now, what's this you were saying about Camus?') . . . .

One reason why I was so remiss in giving thanks was that Francis MacManus's authenticating words, combined with Chris's devotion to, at all costs, learning journalism, had given me my greatest brainwave yet, an idea which was a dead cert and which I considered proof positive of the not-always-obvious virtues of being out on my own and having to think for myself. I wrote to Uncle Seamus. (Actually, I wrote to Granny Royce first to see if it would be okay to contact him. I knew she would read accurately between the lines and butter him up for me.) My plan was, I considered, both the simplest and most perfect embodiment yet of my genius. Uncle Seamus had fought in 1916, right? *The Irish Press* was Dev's paper, right? *Ergo*, what could be more natural than for my grand-uncle to get me a job in his old pal's business? Across this *pons asinorum* I was prepared to be pulled, head high – not snoot-cockingly high, mind, since I had heard severe denunciations of pull, in my time: just high enough to let the inevitable gaggle of begrudging onlookers know that I, for one, was not ashamed of my past or of the rewards rightly accruing to it. Where would any of us be without the likes of Seamus Doyle? Wherever it was, it occurred to me that it might not be too far away from my present station: I didn't want to go there. (Might it not bear the nebulously, though incontrovertibly, inimical name of England?)

The old school ties (Lincoln Gaol, class of '17) had become perhaps a little moth-eaten and musty over the years for want of an air, but their fabric and pattern came from a stern weave and before long ('they took their bloody time,' I muttered) here I was with another mistered letter, pewtery notepaper 113 this time – one of the more obscure of the forty shades of green – the company's symbol, with the large scaly thing, presiding over the title (the eagle of truth or some similar monstrosity from the comic-book times before Christ). And would I be so kind as to come for an interview; please telephone Mr Trainor in the Personnel Department. That was a famous name, too, Trainor, and wasn't personnel a beautiful, modern word – just like electronics, really, in its way. This was it, surely to God: let rainbow now disperse and Bovril lights go dark, my hands were stretching towards the crock of gold, and words, and all the mythic tools of life (O Eagle!).

I was so confident that made-man would henceforth be my middle name that I told Ken what I was doing. 'Good idea,' Ken said. 'I'm afraid there really isn't much of a future for you here. In fact, to be honest, I'm thinking of letting you go at Christmas.' 'Damn good of you, Ken,' I said complacently; I'd just been given three months' notice; Santa was coming early this year. 'And for goodness sake,' said Ken, 'spruce yourself up; wear a tie, get that white shirt washed.' I only laughed, tickled by his mother-hennishness (I prefer now not to recall what I must have looked like – just like a messenger-boy, I suppose); didn't he believe me that it was in the bag? But, because I would be going back to work after the interview, I did have the Swastika do the shirt, and I put my school tie on, hoping that Mr Trainor would recognise it and introduce school as a conversation piece, so I could give him an earful of my editorial style – oh, wouldn't I thunder!

Nothing of the sort took place of course. Mr Trainor was a soft-spoken man: no plaid jacket, no cigar, more inclined to teach than tyrannize. He listened, without remark, to what I had to say, prodding me along (quite needlessly, I thought, needled) with a question or two. What sort of reporting was I interested in? I told him eagerly that book-reviewing appealed – or no, reviewing pictures, make that – my father's in the Film Society! At the moment I was working for? Oh, and what did I think of? – a competitor's name came up. 'Rubbish,' said I: it was, too; sloughed through weak developer, run off on a dirty glazer, 'that glazer should be Brillo'd every day if you don't want spotty snaps.' I mouthed Ken's charge to me, his attempt to justify a very tiresome chore. Later, when I told Ken my remarks about the competition, his jaw dropped and his eyes narrowed: 'Oh God, you didn't, did you?' 'But it's true,' I said: and wasn't that what the *Press* on its masthead said it stood for, *The Truth in the News*? 'I know,' Ken said. 'But they'll think you heard it from me.' 'But I didn't!' Ken sighed, 'I know . . . Shit, anyway.'

Another inner meaning – well *fuck* it, anyhow – it was as bad as religion with its accidents and essences. And this time I knew what I meant by 'it', the whole, dumbfounding, autonomous, institutional, impersonal machinery of man and affairs – the world of work, the world of business, the world of buildings, the immense and indifferent world of the not-me. I wasn't going to be even a messenger-boy for the *Press*. Mr Trainor had explained it all to me. The phrase 'Manning agreement' came into it; the word 'union': he mentioned in passing a bright young fellow fresh out of Coláiste Mhuire who had just been taken on. I understood there never had been a job. But hadn't he heard what Francis MacManus said? 'Of course there will be an opening again next year,' said Mr Trainor, meaning to be kind. 'I'm not sure I'll be around,' I said, not sure what I meant. I saw Christmas, then a wall of snow: I wasn't getting through.

So, I couldn't write. Antonioni could sleep sound. No pen of mine would patronize *La Notte*. Not that I expected to appear on the arts page right away. I'd imagined that they'd test me on the mean streets first, where the drunk and disorderly had their daily sabbath; where the ambulances raced to Jervis Street and cars plunged into the river. I knew the world was a terrible place. But I would make a different world of it (the pen is mightier than the sword). I might even get to like that kind of work: 'Streetwalker – Blood is my Beat'. I could go in for a bit of sleuthing on the side. I could change my name to Cheyney Chandler. Brother of Nancy Drew. The third Hardy boy, the older one, tortured to death by Commies on assignment. Instead, as brooding made me understand, it was goodbye to the free ticket and the big event, goodbye to novelty and fashion and everything the city stood for. Whichever way I stuck a cigarette in my face would never, I knew now, be the city desk way. And why was it that the longer I lived in Dublin the farther away from me it seemed? That must be, I thought, from being on foot so much: I never should have left the buses.

And all the room in Leinster Road had come to mean was that I now lived a private life, and I never had done that before – life had always been something on the outside, on Lismore's streets, in school, even in the family. That outside had somehow been misplaced – with work, I thought (bad luck to it!). I was appalled to realize that here I was in Dublin and there was no swim of things. Failed son of Sundrive!

Failed heir of Enniscorthy, too, this squabble of contents answering to my name, longing for a rectifying image to be imposed on them . . . . This, too, I understood myself to be, in the post-*Press* bout of uncomfortable, unfamiliar introspection. But then, I'd found no thrill on Vinegar Hill. That outcrop of miserable historical associations stood bleak and bare above the pleasant town, a reminder that no matter how nice a time I was having, it was being had against a melancholy background. It wasn't only that in this town my mother was buried, and where her father (also at an early age) had died, and that for an hour every summer as a child I became a graveside mourner, provider of sweet pea and impatiens from Uncle Seamus's garden, exterminator of disrespectful dandelions. Such bitterness, such failures, being final, seemed somehow acceptable. They were, after all, what the past was all about. They made me think that I was right to want to live – to laugh and turn on Luxembourg; to play the piano half the night at dances like my Aunt Chrissy. But there was nobody in Enniscorthy like her. That was what preyed on me, particularly since – heroes and patriots all – who better had the right to vital life than they, and who lacked one more?

In the forty years since his glorious incarceration, all Uncle Seamus had done, it seemed, was cultivate flowers and disappointment. His wife, Aunt Gret, taught school in outlying areas – Taghmon, Tombrack. Seamus read the *Press* and growled and shook his fine white mane. Why was he so unhappy? He didn't have a care in the world; a good woman waited on him hand and foot; though childless, couldn't he rejoice in the little boys and girls in school around, his wife's life? Cultivating roses was his passion. Perhaps he had no faith in ordinary life, its daily pageant pale compared to the historical extravaganza to which he had given his youth. I hesitate to say. What comes to mind is nothing so fanciful as an explanation. Rather it's something sterile, iceberg-silent . . .

it's a cultural hunger-strike. It's the solemn kitsch of the prayerbook he gave me for Confirmation with its snow-white plastic cover and elaborate inscription in Irish. It's the niece he more or less adopted and educated for nunhood. It's the visit he paid in his declining years to his old comrade Dev, now President, and far gone in age. I hear them discuss crops, the numerous recent deaths among the old guard. But very soon they kneel – it's the Glorious Mysteries today. Not very far away, an urchin pries open the side-window of a Morris Minor, reaches in, takes the camera . . . The old men shudder ('what was that?'), clutch their rosary beads with renewed tenacity: 'is now and ever shall be,' the quavery voices conclude. Faith of our fathers, purging and purging . . . .

There were no other men. Seamus had a comrade, and a brother-in-law, Mike Moran, but I don't remember him, except he seemed more energetic, more forward-looking, had a hardware and electrical business in Castle Street – and a family, too, unlike Seamus and Gret. Mrs Moran was Auntie Nell. She had a soft, white face. Her voice was soft and low; contralto. When I climbed the stairs up from the shop and opened the living-room door, she leapt up with gleaming eyes, as though proclaiming, 'Ah, it's fondness that's the true history!' Yet she, too, in her time, like her three sisters, had done her bit for the cause, was a woman, or at least a volunteer in the name of freedom. The four Comerfords – Gret, Nell, Poll and Annie: an extraordinary quartet of high-thinking, risk-taking, God-fearing, Erin-loving girls.

And of course Nell also knew – as who could not – that their day had not quite lasted, the body's destiny too had to be lived out, not just (alas?) the spirit's. There was family, there was the different freedom children have to claim, more fundamental, less idealistic, finally perhaps assuming ideological shape (a language; an unfamiliar, disconcerting language, pronouncing 'Jesus Christ' differently, also 'let' and 'go') in order to receive a hearing. Jim was at sea, radio officer. Willy worked in Wexford town. He had a large family. Eily lived up the street, near the Duffrey. She had a large family, the Askins. They went to Dagenham when the Mac Smile blade factory was shut down. Dispersal. Uprootedness. Jim came back, then went away again. Willy, with family, returned to Enniscorthy: I wasn't able to see why. The wife of Nick White the busman   117 lived in Dublin. May, the nun, professed in Broadstairs. (Uncle Seamus paddled in the English Channel, glowering at the prospect of being snapped. He did not wear the bottom of his trousers rolled.) Michael Moran, youngest son, became an Augustinian, vowing poverty. He was ordained in Valladollid. That was how it went in those days: sunderings and surrenders. Restlessness. No different from ourselves in Lismore. Family life a tunnelling through to exits.

Except that in Lismore I was aware of the exertions: I heard the slamming doors, the inadmissible language. In Enniscorthy all I met was sweet gentleness and generosity. It was as if the women who stayed were happy accepting all that came their way without complaint, living in an Ireland masked by the other cheek, incurious legatees of a two-faced heritage. Why weren't they nurses, teachers, barmaids, actresses? Why hadn't the world made of them what they so clearly were entitled to be? It bothered me. Their natures were richer than their lives. It weighed on me, that row-free passive tolerance which seemed as close to happiness as anything I'd seen adults manage: why did it make me sad? (Impossible questions. Impossible to reconstruct and deconstruct those far-off atmospheres and auras. And equally impossible to forget. Impressions all the more indelible for being inchoate, resistant to all prompts towards meaning; watery sunbeams in the eternal parlour of those endless afternoons . . . . Hauntings.)

And Anne, Granny Royce, embodying it all. She was about five feet, with thin blonde hair. She married William. He died. They named their one child Nuala. She died. Granny owned a house in town where I was born. She had to let it go. She lived in Pullinstown on the farm with her uncle, fierce whiskey Joe. We fed the hens, we picked the winesaps in the orchard. Andy Doolin at the end of the boreen brought honeycombs (they looked as brains should look). When we could see Mount Leinster in the distance it was a good sign. In the evenings the cards for spoil fifteen; the oil-lamp's mellow light. Joe died. The farm went, so back to town. Declining years. She lodged with able Gret and grumpy Seamus, drew her pension, kept forgetfully putting smouldering fag-butts in her handbag 'for after', became a risky visitor. She never saw enough of her darling grandson – the stranger, the survivor, all she had to show, poor thing. Her life of loss. Her sunniness.

After the *Press* episode, she contrived an invitation for us both to some old friends. I did enough overtime for a five-day weekend. The friends lived in south County Wexford, less than thirty miles from Enniscorthy; of course we could have got there, but she insisted on breaking the journey to them and staying the night at White's Hotel in Wexford town. We sat up late talking, smoking. I carried on loud and long that nothing was going right. Everything was rotten. Nobody gave a damn. I was sick of it. Musha, musha, she, as ever, soothed, not wanting to hear my crass goodbye to Enniscorthy, home of grand deeds, and useless articles. My loss her greater loss; my hurt to her more painful than to me. Eventually I shut up, submitting with ill-grace to her mild insistence that it was a shame, and hard to understand, but these things are sent to try us, but please God, next year . . . . As I had in the *Press* office, however, I had an unsettling inkling that there was no next year. Suddenly it seemed that I was in this impersonal room not to regroup but to part. In one lengthening silence, where only wreaths of smoke expressed our transitory presence, I saw that we had been attending each other's wake.

III

A SWIM IN THE CANAL

1

It was from no less an authority than Mam I had it that dancing defined pleasure. There were no Paul Jones's now, of course, she sighed, no Lancers. But God be with the days when the Courthouse was a flood of frocks and polish. The army band came down from Fermoy (I had seen the shell of its burned barracks from the train: the barrack square had made a fine foundation for the hurling field . . .). The military two-step was executed to perfection: 'Now everybody "Sing bum ta-ra-ra", it's that ever-popular polka, "Roll Out the Barrel".' Miss O'Shea's workroom, where Mam was a seamstress, was agog with muslin ruffs and furbelows. God be with the days. All you found now at dances, she lamented, were clowns in blue suits and brown shoes, people who were crippled from lifetimes in wellingtons and showing off in court shoes with masochistic cuban heels ('what possessed her – wasn't her mother a martyr to fallen arches?'), not to mention the trollops who attended just to be noticed – there seemed to be heinzery of them, if not more than fifty-seven varieties. They sounded especially interesting to me: it was a fine, fat, dirty word, trollop.

Even if standards had declined, however, there was still no mistaking dances' importance. There was one for every important day of the year – Cappoquin Regatta, Tallow Horse Fair, Race night, Stephen's night, the night of the gymkhana. They were the equal and opposite, it seemed, of holy days of obligation, secular sabbaths, responding with licence and late hours to the duties of observance, a reciprocity seemingly confirmed by the fact that the same clothes were worn to kneel and to do the Highland fling. Not that the occasion need be so formal. Outside Lismore, at the Araglen crossroad, there was 123 an open-air stage. On summer evenings, in the gloaming, town lads would glide with country lasses, Tom Keating obliging on the button accordion. But a stop was put to it. I remember the talk it caused at the time. My uncle Georgie foamed, but I thought the priests were right: you could get your death of cold, staying out like that. It was only a lot later I found out the stage was an occasion of sin, and I was already in Dublin with pretensions to paycocking my way around the Four Provinces Ballroom, Harcourt Street, before I found myself, like George no doubt, in furious pursuit of that same great sin.

The dances which took place at big events were not the only opportunities to shake a leg and show a tail feather. As I knew from Aunt Chrissy, who played for the Marino, the Lismore band, there were dances of all shapes and sizes. They were held in galvanized-iron sheds, in concrete blockhouses known as Parish Halls and frequently named after some attribute of the Blessed Virgin. The Marino played Conna, Knockanore, Ballycotter, Kilworth: once I remember Chrissy saying the following morning – she was up to get our breakfasts as usual – they'd got lost en route the night before, stopped for directions, were told merely to follow the electricity poles: where they ended the band was supposed to be. They'd play from nine to one, nine to two, or just a hop, till midnight. Then pack the car and again home in darkness by roads that weaved with hallucinatory, lightless bicycles. Sometimes, if the dance was an all-out effort to raise money for the hurling-club, say, sisters of the committee-members would be recruited to make sandwiches, slice Swiss-roll and serve tea. Chrissy, too busy playing to take the floor much, appraised the evenings in terms of the patrons' drunkenness and the lavishness of the spread, the latter a code for *two* kinds of sandwiches (ham and corned beef), the former secret lingo for whether she'd met anybody she wouldn't mind meeting again – maybe he'd cycle over to a hurling match some Sunday soon . . . .

At least I assumed her pleasure could not be solely governed by eating and non-drinking, much less by her share of the band's take (a pair of shoes and a large Gold Flake is probably as much as that amounted to). There had to be romance as 124 well, though it wasn't Chris but Sally, a Church Lane neighbour, who best bore that necessity in mind. Wherever the band went, Sal went too, emerging – a cumulo-nimbus in her early thirties; a woman for whom the word 'blouse' was designed – from her little house into the promise of evenings in whatever the feminine was of 'all Gillette and heel-ball', Mam's phrase for freshly shaved, brilliantined, date-conscious men, a phrase applied ironically to people for whose state of mind irony was instant deflation and death. So here she came in American regalia – she had relatives in Massashootus, as she said: ensembles of fuchsia, turquoise, tangerine; of salmon, cinnamon, heliotrope – the nosegay that ate Boston. And always given to having a superb good time. Each outing kept her talking until the identical next one. Each time she danced the whole night through with a series of smashing fellas, every man of whom was a creamery manager. A faraway look would enter her small eyes, her face would sag a little (revealing incipient flabbiness), as she pictured herself once more in the capable arms of a stocky citizen hitting forty – he lied, of course, but Sal could tell; she simpered from being lied to; she loved his comforting scent of evaporated milk . . . . She came to tell it all to Chrissy. I stood apart, humming and pretending not to hear her, but secretly exulting in the news of this dancing life. So grown-ups did have fun, it seemed: their always seeming fraught became less distressing – an act put on for children, probably, so that we would be good.

At school there was dancing too – apart from the Irish kind, that is, which wasn't worth bothering about because it failed to feature partners in the personal, modern, accessible sense of the term. There was non-traditional as well: a woman with wattles taught me to tango. I was nothing loth, being at this point in Fourth Year and able to boast, in the idiom of the inmates, that I knew I didn't have it for stirring me tay: dancing was going to be awful handy one of these fine summers . . . . The lessons, however, were lacking. Music, for one thing. Rather than turn our heads with the wrong translation altogether of Latin, the powers that be evidently, and correctly, concluded that counting would never make us prey to passion. So it was a quick one-two-three up and down the clearing provided for us at the back of the assembly hall, a space so devoid of atmosphere that it would have quelled the call of any and all concupiscence. I was told I had good rhythm.

I wondered if I'd recognize the compliment in Spanish – clearly the object of the 'extra' was to ensure we would behave like gentlemen if ever invited to an embassy do in Buenos Aires.

Tangos had no relevance to our Saturday-night school hops, that was plain. But then those hops bore no very clear relation to what we thought a dance was, particularly with just each other or a priest as partner, an arrangement all the more ridiculous since the boarders of the Mercy Convent were no more than the height of a wall away. (This wall was like all the others, of course, topped with either spikes or broken glass whose ugliness kept fresh thoughts of world, flesh and devil, while inhibiting actions that might relieve thought's burdens.) So instead of lurching daintily with a heifer in a gymslip – it was safer, broadly speaking, to disdain what could not be attained – we scraped the floor together, released the odd roar together. Stubbles, ace accordionist of Kildysart, did his best to satisfy all tastes, from Bridie Gallagher's blockbuster, 'The Boys from County Armagh', to Slim Dusty's great epic, 'A Pub With No Beer', while for the modern set (whom nothing would satisfy, according to the glares of their keepers), 'Wooden Heart' and 'Blueberry Hill'. He refused to give us 'Lipstick on Your Collar'.

The priests spun round sedately, prefects firmly in tow, giving good example. The rest of us fell over one another, giggling, cursing, talking dirty to our dirty-talking dates; the few man-and-wife couples, as we called them, turned into wallflowers and ardently conversed; Rock Sullivan looked in vain for someone to jive with; Stubbles caught us unawares by throwing in, out of the blue, 'The Lion Sleeps Tonight', or bored out of his mind, a stave or two of a reel or a jig. Which was great. It reminded us that dancing was one of the faiths of our fathers. Gaels did it. Priests did it. We would do it too, properly, indelibly, to the tune of 'Here Comes Summer', 'A White Sportscoat and a Pink Carnation', the revised lyric of 'Peggy Sue' never far from our minds.

> Oh Peggy Sue, I do love you,
> Especially in your nightie.
> When moonlight flits across your tits –
> Oh, Jesus Christ Almighty!

Refreshed by renewed resolve – there could only be a future –
we trooped off to night prayers.

Like a lot of other things in my life, however, dancing at first
turned out to be only in theory: when it came to the real thing,
I was missing. At least that was what happened when the first
dance for which I was eligible took place, a dance that was a
must for everyone, the victory céilí.

The novelty was not only in having the céilí but in having
something to celebrate. But we did indeed, and we knew how
to be grateful for it. We would dance. The whole town would
dance. The Courthouse floor would never be the same. It was
the summer I was fifteen, when Da and Kay vacationed in
America for the first time and the Lismore minor hurling team
won the Western division of the country championship,
crushing Tallow, hammering Ballinameela. . . We had all
suddenly come together as a generation, had laid claim to our
bodies, were history in the making. I was allowed to come
along to carry the bottle and the spare sticks, to roar myself
hoarse, a kind of outsize, overzealous mascot, the team's
uncomical version of romancing, dancing Sally from Church
Lane. Oh, was I happy!

We beat Fourmilewater in the final, which was played in the
Fraher Field, Dungarvan, no less – a prestigious venue
particularly since it was the first pitch we'd played on that
wasn't let for grazing between fixtures, thus was neither
covered with cowcakes nor riddled with sheep's raisins, so
players could run and fall without circumspection and
without risking what parents greatly feared, lockjaw. And
every man among us played a blinder: Tommy Heffernan,
Gunner Brady, Paddy Farrell, John O'Connor, Peter Hickey . .
. lithely skipping through the twilight, pale forms amid the
lengthening shadows, light failing beyond the homes of the
Colligan Rockies and Brickey Rangers, a coaster's masts
framing Maloney's warehouse – inscriptions of an evening
that has yet to end.

And famous warriors, guests of honour at the dance, that
other way of saying the body was temporarily okay. The three
beautiful daughters of Johnny Jawsus Murphy were there.
Martha Dunne was there too. The Fleming girls, as well, no
doubt. And who knows what went on. The lads tipped one

another winks next day; the more they did so, the more credulous I became. So it wasn't called the Courthouse for nothing. All I knew was that I hadn't been allowed to go. It was bad enough, apparently, that I was smoking: now I wanted five shillings for a dance. Wasn't I turning into the right little maneen . . . ? I prowled the streets. I heard the old accordions playing . . . . 'The Rose of Mooncoin', 'Red Sails in the Sunset'. Latecomers passed me hurrying, their people having finally relented, calling 'Are you going?' to me. I was used to feeling strange, to offering explanations of myself, at school, in Dublin. But I never had felt strange in Lismore till then. The feeling was a victory of sorts, I suppose, though not for me.

It wasn't until some time later (I may have already been in Dublin and long-weekending in Lismore with Peg to lick my Monkstown wounds) that I discovered that strange was how dances were supposed to feel. One of the lads still at home, whom I didn't know drove, much less had a car, borrowed a relative's old Anglia – and here was I arriving back in a Fiat whose front I could barely tell from its back: was it possible that there was someone in Lismore freer and more trusted than I (shades of the céilí flapped unsettlingly before me)? But such thoughts didn't linger. I was too taken with the forty-five m.p.h. dash along familiar roads, familiar figures on familiar bikes waving in the dust after us. By the time we reached that failed but welcome Courthouse, Dungarvan Town Hall, I was racing as fast as the car, plonked down with lordly (citified, I thought) aplomb my six-and-a-tanner – which meant that it was not the greatest event on West Waterford's social calendar that year: big dances cost at least seven-and-six – and made like a sheep through a gap for the dark place where the saxes wailed.

Oh, what a night that was. At one point I was in a ring of six or eight skipping to a Johnny and the Hurricanes medley. The floor was a burning trampoline. The body was a pogo stick. I had never sweated so much in my life before. Oh, what delicious hell was this? And though the circling and the skipping seemed to go on for a long time, when it ended all I wanted was the same thing over again. But the music slowed. Then that was all right too, though. The singer poured himself into the mike, doing Ruby and the Romantics' 'Our Day Will Come'. It was then I learned how to move without making forward progress, without caring if there never was progress again, because all that mattered was the sandy shuffle of the brushes on the snare drum, the girl's hair like a tickling breeze about my face. I saw now why dances had to be crowded; from a full heart I silently thanked the strangers all around me for creating for me, for everyone, this inspirational heat, this fabulous undulance in which we bobbed and dipped, bubbles forming, breaking, forming in richly seething stirabout.

And I found out what 'shift' meant. This was what dates were called in school, and I could never imagine why, since all the word meant was move. I realized that on a date one might well be moved, but the way the term was used suggested more the adventures of the hand than the palpitations of the heart. I supposed it must, like everything else, be a double meaning – connected, perhaps, to mickey muscle rising to the occasion, though (and this was not easy to figure out either) there was no need to be on a date for that to happen. But that evening, as soon as the girl I was dancing with said 'How about a breath of fresh air; I'm stifling', I realized at once that that was my line, except that the way to say it was, 'Will we shift?' disguising in laconic lacking confidence.

There was a bandstand in a little park beyond the dog-legged street. We went there and watched the idle water of the bay, and the moon over the Cunnigar, the sandbank that was silting up the bay but which now seemed as exotic and unthreatening as a sleeping whale. She shivered. She was wearing a cotton blouse, a skirt of navy blue. She was very thin, pinched face that spread just like a child's whenever she smiled (and she liked to smile), arms and legs that looked as though they were just the shoots of real limbs. Her name, she said, was Bríd. She lived in Wolfe Tone Street – did I know where that was? Yes, on the fringe of Loughmore, the poor part, out by the County Home. I asked her who her favourite singer was. She said Cliff Richard. I pretended not to mind. Soon I was more interested in how it was that while her arm was cold and goose-bumped she otherwise felt very warm. I noticed that her lips tasted at first of peppermint, then after a while of strong tea. Lips clung, noses didn't seem to matter: that too seemed to go with the stranger, with the strangeness. And strangest of all: here I was with a girl who'd let me dance most of the night with her without minding one bit the   129 number of times I had to say 'Sorry!' for trampling her.

But I couldn't miss my lift. We danced the evening's last slow waltz, stood with arms around each other for the ragged valediction of the national anthem's final bars, always played at dances and cinemas then to make endings official. How much more pleasant it felt to loll irreverently together . . . it was as though our bodies had finally found the nerve to tell us the good news – you've been solo, uptight at attention, long enough. A last squeeze; her final, goodbye smile. In the glare of the full houselights she looked very white and wan. I didn't care. She was the one. The lads were calling though. (Did life have to go on?) I know: I'll get 'My Happiness' by Connie Francis played for her on Irish Requests on Luxembourg. No – it'd take too long. What, so? 'I'll write to you!' I blurted. I could think of no higher compliment . . . .

And I did write, care of the Dungarvan postmaster, which obtuse Cupid replied re my communication of 2nd inst . . . directed to state . . . *le meas* . . . I waited and waited, but nothing from Bríd. Then, perhaps six months or more later, I got a letter from the Isle of Man. She was a chambermaid in a hotel there: did I remember her . . . ? I saw in her ill-formed hand a thin frame, loneliness, a gruelling slog and screaming bosses, no dancing. The romance of travel: the impoverishment of work. She too now knew, like me, the history of the world. But I didn't know how to write back. I didn't have either the words or the nerve to tell her that if she remembered the dance, that was all that mattered.

I remembered. I went over every step of it often, though not as often as I would have liked, because the distractions of the job, of family, of ambition, of wondering if Dublin was the larger life to addle me, kept falling like so many shadows between the dance and me, supplying a wrong, lugubrious kind of darkness. If only those nuisances would stop putting years on me . . . .

Yet sometimes when I relived the Bríd evening it vaguely struck me as peculiar that I had found it such an eye-opener, or rather, languorous eye-closer – lotus and hookah in the shadow of Helvick. Hadn't I known all about this kind of thing from the time I was a small boy? The dance was unfamiliar rustling and urgent steps upstairs. It was shaving cream on

Sunday night, and scent in the middle of the week. It was Mick Delahunty's twenty-one piece orchestra: Mick Del from Clonmel, as big and brassy as Geraldo or Joe Loss. He even played a Hunt Ball at Lismore Castle – next thing we knew he'd be on the wireless. There wasn't a hall in Munster that band didn't pack, including our very own, the monstrosity clad in russet galvanized iron, the Happydrome (whoever called it that must have thought Hippo-ditto an obscure English joke which he was determined not to fall for: *if it sounds like a zoo they'll turn it into one* . . .). This was what I understood the dance to mean – not understanding anything: peculiar venues, foreign (Tipperary) musicians.

Not only that, the dance meant the morning after, too. While Mam heard Mass at the convent, Chrissy and George would go over every inch of it again, exhausted but, clearly, delightedly at peace. They kept telling me to eat my egg, but I always made a point of listening to this legendary stuff of grown-ups' night-time. The tone was so agreeable – it often was when something shared outside was brought back home. Not that the events were particularly exotic. The footwork of some Ballysaggart bostoon had nearly crippled Chrissy. Geo thought he was going to break his neck at first, the floor had been that heavily massaged with Glideezi. But Andy Ahearne was still a gorgeous dance. Mona, the new girl at the hairdresser's, was found to be 'pleasant, like, y'know, no airs and graces; a natural being' – said wistfully (the workday loomed). For a while, the familiar had ceased to be contemptible. Neighbour met neighbour on an equal footing. There was the harmless lottery of pairing off with partners. Life was both reduced and elevated to a grand game, and all were free to play, all – as far as I could tell – seemed mollified having played, having lapsed, both male and female, indiscriminately, publicly, though without usurping privacy, just once in a way, together, imagining they could share, into the culture of the body. There were faraway looks in early-morning eyes, and absent-minded silences: they told me that the dancers felt they never wanted to feel freer than they did dancing.

And sometimes for a while after a dance, Chris and Geo would try behaving in that freedom's name. Geo would stop going to the library and would hurry off as though he had something better to do. Coming from school I'd see Chris making off down Ferry Lane on her own. I'd run after her, calling: it wasn't fair of her to go walking without me. It was shocking to hear she didn't want me with her – nobody went anywhere alone; who better than I for company? She was being so bad that she was sometimes late for tea. Then – equally shocking – it turned out Geo was doing a strong line with a girl from Tallow. I happened on them, talking earnestly, as I rounded the corner going home one Sunday evening after benediction. I greeted him effusively. He was less than friendly. I hung around, thinking he might give me money, but I was wasting my time. Then, just as I was heading on, he called me. 'Don't tell,' he told me, seriously: 'Don't say you saw me.' But what was there not to tell? He was doing nothing. Not long afterwards he returned to normal, reading Westerns by the dozen, staggering after midnight on the stairs: we knew where we were with him again then. A good thing he'd given up trying to have a private life, a life beyond the family: that kind of thing only happened in pictures, and they weren't real. Didn't Geo know no dance went on forever?

He would have only got in trouble by carrying on. Priest trouble – there was always that. Every so often the chapel would resound with denunciations of immorality, late nights, motor cars, modern ways that forgot God, but let those selfish enough to think of nothing but pleasure take care in case God forgot them! I understood the bit about the cars. Priests were very nearly the only unmarried people who owned them. Naturally they didn't want anyone going the roads to have one and that way start getting it into their heads that they were as well off as the clergy . . . . As for the rest, the roaring could sometimes be exhilarating.

True trouble, though, and what I was really afraid of was that my erring uncle and my wayward aunt would be mentioned in Pot Pourri, the paragraph of rumour and innuendo that appeared in the 'Lismore Notes' carried weekly by the *Dungarvan Leader* (the pot was pronounced pott, as though to underline the fact that the paragraph's intention was to stew certain reputations in gossipers' acidulous salivations). Full names were never used, just first name initials or identification by means of place. 'The Chapel Street colleen wouldn't be pleased if she saw the couple that went up the

132

Green Road Thursday evening . . . . A little bird told me that Paddy F – is off his grub on account of the new employee at the Hotel . . . . ' All good clean fun; mostly made up, perhaps, to cause a stir or give reluctant swains encouragement. It was all so much trouble – meeting someone, finding enough time for them, finding a place to be with them. But I remember, too, that people got upset if a scenario could be said to frame them. Talk of this kind – Miss Emptyhearts speaks the language of love, unsweet nothings – would be awful if it came our way. We'd die of shame. Safer by far to dance and have done.

2

There was the Crystal in South Anne Street. I won a spot prize there. The singer stopped the music suddenly and called 'Who recorded that one?' Quick as a flash I called back, 'Cliff Richard'. (Easy – 'The Young Ones'). Two tickets to the Wednesday hop was my reward. My dancing partner was so impressed she almost let me date her.

There was the Town and Country Club in Parnell Square, but it was too far to walk back from. So was the National, which was also somewhere thereabouts. I didn't go there either. I'd heard it was a home-on-the-range kind of place with quare culchie cowboys and the quickstep a thundering herd, or perhaps I read as much in the raw redness of its neon sign. Dancehall signs should be pink, the delicacy in red's desire: they should be green, the colour of hope in the liturgy.

Mainly, though the Four Provinces in Harcourt Street was my delight and especially the Sivilkems of a Friday night. That was the easiest to walk home from. If you clicked it would more than likely be with some bird from southside flatland, so taxiing her back would not break the bank. And it was best to score on Friday night, obviously, since there would still be cash enough for Sunday night at the pictures, if she was interested, and of course she would be interested in getting something for nothing, who wouldn't? Even I, prone to regard 133 myself as the Lazarus of Leinster Road (compared to the large family of civil servant Dives I saw around me), took care to have spondulicks for the weekend. Dining off a small tin of, for preference, Crosse & Blackwell spaghetti greatly helped the cause, I found, and if on the toasted rounds of O'Rourke's Vienna I was able to shed temporarily the Lazarine for the Lucullan – there had to be an image always, something that the world poured into me to salve all the hungers.

The Sivilkems was best, too, because it was a student dance – put on by prospective civil and chemical engineers. The Ags – the civil-chems' agricultural equivalents in academe – probably had the better dances; they usually had all the big-name bands, anyway, and a more exalted-sounding venue, the Olympic. But that hall was obscurely located somewhere off the upper reaches of Heytesbury Street, the dances were dearer, and in any case were mid-week events, suggesting that their public was the student élite, lazy buggers all, privileged to stay in bed as late as they liked all the live-long week. Dances existed to eliminate distinctions between their patrons, or at least to make the jeopardy of difference negotiable – a rehearsal for the dutiful sublimations of parochial whist drives in later life: Mrs V. Mooney all night upping the ante on biddable Mr Tommy Dunne. But it was hard not to be aware of the distinctions.

Why dances were the remit of students, I don't know. I suppose it helped the dancehall owner identify a clientele. But I doubt he hired students to run dances for him. And I don't remember any talk about what happened to proceeds and profits. Was something of the take used to help fund scholarships for scholars barred by poverty rather than by brainlessness from college? Was the whole business nothing more than a handy grind in the entrepreneurship without which success in later life would be inconceivable? I don't know. Money, presumably, came into it somewhere. Anyone with only public spirit could try doing the St Vincent de Paul Society's sober cakewalk.

The main point about student dances, however, was that they had the best women, drawn by career prospects for themselves – good catches, that is; well-educated, well-paid professionals. Why else would they go? Therefore, certain vital steps had to be taken in order to compete with bestness.

A brisk rubdown, first. Bathing would have been better, of course, but a bath cost a shilling, the price of a mineral later on, and a mineral was essential because you had to have something to sweat; besides, if negotiations were going so poorly as to recommend sleep before midnight, at least a shilling would have been saved towards the cigarettes essential to easing the empty stomach from Thursday lunch to Friday pay. Then, after Matt-Talbotizing myself with a towel that felt like a luge along a course of pebble-dashing, came the ticklish part: the shave. Even if it took half the evening, the shave had to be perfect. I still was far from shaving nick-free, so was unable to shave without smoking, which caused problems of its own, but smoke did manage to impart the cool within which its more gelid cousin, lather, was supposed to produce on the outside. With a fag going I at least had an image of the way things should go. The slightest sign of blood meant trouble, though, because since the *Press* episode I'd boycotted newspapers, hence had nothing to plug a leak (Mrs O'Connell's jax-paper was non-staunching, shiny Izal), and it was most unwise to let the damage congeal by itself since standing, watching, waiting, wondering, foot-tapping, made it all too easy (I could vouch for it) absently, fretfully to pick the cicatrice and find yourself B.D. (bloodied dimple), much more objectionable – much less deniable (I could vouch for it) – than the mentionable social scourge – B.O. Thus, I scrupulously shaved.

Ditto quiffed. But this I knew from primary school, when Brother Blake used to give points for neat writing, good sumsmanship and tidy appearance in which smart hairdo rated highly. Whoever got points had no slaps next day, at least we could more or less completely take charge of the hair-control component of our destiny. When it came to quiffs, therefore, I knew exactly which way the wind blew. Ignoring, though with difficulty, the insipid displays of hispidity on chest, in oxter, and in any case knowing of no lubricant which would increase and multiply same, I devoted assiduous attention to the mane that mattered, the visible one. Here again, as with the fickle blade, great care, or to give care its proper name, Brylcreem, was called for: too much and it might run when the hall began to swelter, ruining the shirt not worn since Sunday, and worse, causing excessive use of hanky which risked making the partner think she was dancing with a cosmetic cripple suffering from a progressive and evidently degenerative attack of leaky pores and semaphores. (Partners were invariably, irresistibly, maddeningly impeccable.)

No blood anywhere; no soap in ear folds? Okay. Tie; jacket; pat of pocket for key and smokes. Right. Time to take the floor (please God, tonight's the night . . .). Time to hit the high spots, where- and whatever they were. Time to enter real time. The preparations had to climax in the front door being slammed, that irrevocable moment, point of no return, a subconscious rehearsal of the emergences and turning points which, it was hoped, the evening would present, which indeed the preparations – *pas seul*, Narcissus and his porcelain trough – were intended to excite, that sole self a dance of possibility, leading (being led by) that machine which called dreams to test, the dancehall, where with luck and timing leg might inadvertently slide along anonymous leg, and give rise to the thrilling little kick and tingle.

Sweet mystery of life! I'd found at last what it was all about: people not being people, but being girls. Birds, dames, wimmin, dolls, dishes, bikes, cushy pushers with dainty dairies, quims, gowls, fans, and diddies. Pleasure machines. Hot. Fast. They were girt about with hooks and hawsers, but they wouldn't be long shifting your gears for you, and their arses were upholstered like Rolls-Royces, the better, it was said, to give a good ride. I was more surprised than disappointed, however, when I discovered that many girls seemed to wear cardboard covers over their behinds. These inhibitors – were they corsets? – meant as little to me as the placards outside black churches in Leeson Park and Adelaide Road, roaring in big letters about the wages of sin and judgment that is at hand. At hand: but I only knew those rears in reverse, from dancefloor collisions.

The female and the feminine were a lingo all their own, and were only known by what was said of them, the jokes, the slang. One whore says to the other, 'D'ya smoke after it?' The other one says, 'I dunno: I never looked.' I'd heard lads in school say that the reason our tubby matron, Miss Dooley, was in a bad mood was because she had the rags on. But I was afraid to ask what they were (better pretend to know it all than to be laughed at). And even if I knew I still didn't know it all, I was at least beyond the stage of sneaking up to the library in Lismore to check the big dictionary for the meaning of spermatoza. I knew a fair few of the facts. It was life that was still a little obscure.

A girlfriend, though, would surely help me in all respects. Dublin could hardly deny me that much: with all the gorgeous girls there were, wasn't there a Molly Malone for me (where are you, sweet Miss Kelly?). There had better be. I was the one just about dying of a fever. It wouldn't have particularly bothered me if girls really were dolls, devoid of crankcases and headlights. I'd respect them, I'd renounce for life all the passionate kissing and close embracing that Catholic Truth Society pamphlets warned against, I'd make a weekly confession of my non-sins to their experts on such matters, Daniel Lord, S.J., I'd do anythng (meaning nothing) just for a friendly face and merry eyes.

I had plenty of time to wonder about the everything and nothing of my dancehall days, to wonder: was it my imagination or did Chris and George have a springier step after their long rewarding walks without me; and about the night with Bríd, when everything seemed so casually happy (what had casualness to do with happiness, tell me?). Bríd – I should have stayed in Dungarvan with her: now the girls I danced with never had names. I never knew what to say after 'Fierce crowd. Great band.' If I asked them where they were from, it only led to greater silence: what did I know of Edenderry or Bennettsbridge? And I knew girls were not supposed to talk first. There now, verbal me, who'd virtually talked Chris into needing a hearing aid .... Wasn't it terrible, I said to myself, that Camus, smart as he was, and calm, and George Orwell, so brusque and clean, had nothing to offer me in this line? Was that how it had to be though – Chris for talk and a pretty kisser for dancenights?

So all too often, when it came time for 'He'll Have to Go', I was in the balcony sucking fiercely on yet another cigarette, feeling that I was the one who had to go, that the whole thing was a dead loss – Jim Reeves, for God's sake! Couldn't they do any better than that President of the Unctuous Schmaltz of America? Yes! – not only were the girls not forthcoming, the bands didn't give a damn. They played the popular, pure-in-

137

heart dead man; made him one of our own. Didn't they know there was a dance revolution going on? As Johnny Tillotson had so eloquently reminded the free peoples of the world, it was the age of 'Poetry in Motion' (the motion being a girl's, the poetry being her motion) or, to put it another way, like Chubby Checker, 'It's Pony Time!' But if it wasn't the twist – idiot, passé offspring of the hoolahoop – it wasn't anything at all: 'We'd like to pick the tempo up now, ladies and gentlemen, boys and girls, with the latest from Helen Shapiro: 'Walking Back to Happiness'. *Walking*! Where was the Fly, the Mashed Potato, the Madison, the Hitchhiker, the Locomotion, the Watusi – 'Let's do the wa-wa-tusi!' – by the exciting Watusis?

Not that rickety me required the latest dance fad to appreciate a band. Even without a radio, I was still more hip, more cool than anyone else – I knew that for a fact (not knowing very many people). Nobody had my awe and admiration for Santo and Johnny's 'Sleep Walk'; The Teddybears' 'To Know Him Is to Love Him' (now that was how a holy anthem should sound, instead of lapsed marches like as 'Faith of Our Fathers'); and breathed there a man with soul so dead who never to himself had said 'This is fucking beautiful', about Maxine Brown's 'All in My Mind'? It didn't matter which band it was – Rebel Cork's own Dixielanders; the Clipper Carlton of Strabane, who took the country completely unawares by coming over the border and playing like men possessed – were they invaders to be suspicious of or escaped prisoners of conscience (minor musical Mindzentys to be welcomed)? Even the Royal itself: nobody knew more than me, felt more than me. Too good is what I was (probably): signs on I was being kept to the sideline. But the fools, the fools! . . . the bands, by not giving me my due, were only drawing attention to themselves.

I pitied them, really. They weren't even young. How could they be? No Mammy would allow a son to travel and be out late unless he was well into his twenties. Their taste had to be formed by different dancing, perhaps even by pre-teen ditties from Guy Mitchell and Max Bygraves. And they hardly believed in electricity at all: reed and horn still basically ruled their roost. They seemingly disdained the perfection of the blessed plastic wafer created by the grace of electronics. They rejected the high calling of being human radios. They only played the tunes. They didn't mean them. It never occurred to them that they shouldn't be so innocent. They should have paid more attention to Messiah Kennedy, to his prophets Elvis and Jerry Lee. Ask not what your jukeboxes can do for you but what you can do for your jukeboxes. They should have got to know me. I'd sing. My name is Frankie Avalon (open-neck white shirt, collar up). I'm going to do my new song, 'Venus'. I want to sing it as though Villon wrote it ('Tant crie l'on Noel qu'il vient' . . .), but I don't know how. Besides, I really don't want to be Avalon-sweet. I want to be city-burning mad. I want to go *I'm free / let me play / let me play / I'm free*, like an angry jazzman (the man that rock forgot) shouting out the crime of his frustrations. Put your sweet lips, ooh-whee honey, do-it do-it, a little, just a little, little – Ho! tickles, umm nice; tickles – haha-hohoho-HEE! Whoa! Is that the phone – god *damn* that pho-o-no-o-no-one . . . !

Oh well, here we go again. Friday night, it's better than being on my own isn't it (but I *am* on my own). Fierce crowd, d'you like the band?

'I'm from Tallow,' she said.

'What?!' I bawled, screeching to a halt in the middle of 'Are You Lonesome Tonight?' (or perhaps 'Poor Shep'), causing a chain of skidding and weaving and muttering, though did I care whose sails I was taking the wind out of? Not with – This was –

And there was more. She was not really from the next town west of Lismore but from a townland in between whose name was inseparable from a couple of lads I knew from there; 'You don't know Paddy and Willy – ?' I shouted. When she told me she was their sister I nearly went through the floor first, then the ceiling. *I believe in God, the Father Almighty* . . . I should have shamed us both by throwing my arms around her and hugging her till surgery us part. This was somebody who knew me! But unabashedly staring at her as though daring her to disappear, as though waiting for myself to wake up, was all I could manage for the time being – though I might readily have realized she was certainly all there from the virtually continual presence of her insteps beneath my feet. I assumed she didn't mind, however, because she said nothing when I, 139 being too distracted, forgot 'Sorry'. Instead, after a while, she disengaged herself from my omnivorous, moronic eyes, and began to giggle.

I came to: be serious, I told myself.

'What's your name?' I gasped.

'Maura.'

I'd never heard a nicer. Simple, yes, but not common; definitely not common . . . Irish, but not off-puttingly so, as Seoirse was. Kind of like Bríd in a way, but nicer, really; much nicer. A name with shape and firmness to it. Not a thin name. A name for a Ritchie Valens hymn.

Now, all of a sudden, the world had become a very small place, consisting simply of merry eyes and unbitten nails. There were well-tended teeth, too, which let me know she was special (not everybody had them). There was a gorgeous globe of chestnut hair. And I could live in the small confines of this world, I thought. Its slow time would be a boon, its minute graduations would never intimidate. I had no need any more to play the secret-life, alternative-self game. I had come home to Tallow. We perpetrated certain phrases to me as we congealed and unglued in the slow, deliriously slow melée. ('Yes,' I said stupidly, 'I love The Cadets'; 'Yes,' Maura said charmingly, 'I do come here fairly often'.) We were Mr and Mrs Crysostomos. 'We'd like to liven it up a little bit, now, with 'Way Down Yonder in New Orleans'. We were Freddy Cannon's *Whoo!*

Then, though, just as my heart was turning into a toasted marshmallow (on fire with sweetness), Maura muttered something apologetic and headed for the sidelines for earnest hugger-mugger with a blonde girl, and at once I greatly feared. Silly me: be *serious*, can't you, I told myself: how can anything go wrong? The whole thing is a miracle: it can't turn out typically. She knows me, I told myself; I know her. We can place each other, we can see each other in lives the opposite of this (she carries a bucket to the hens, I lounge at the Red House corner like a man of the town), our talk is anchored to familiar never-mentioned roads and the bark of saucy mongrels from cottages. She can't leave me down. She knew I was somebody, because she knew the someplace I was from. She couldn't let me down. Yet – damn it to hell and blast it – what was keeping her!

Of course the dance saved me (how could I have doubted it?). A ladies' choice was announced and, promptly, forward Maura came smiling. It was the first time I'd been saved from the ignominy of self-banishment to the balcony, the usual choice that ladies gave me. Now we danced closer. *Put Your Sweet Lips* . . . I didn't have a nerve the soppy number failed to hit. I was captain and master. Plain sailing now. Steady as she goes . . . Aye, aye, sir! Oh *fuck!* the first mate was saluting: down, boy; *down*, sir! (*He'll* have to go.) But the mutinous flesh would not be still. What now?

'It's fierce warm,' I blurted; 'would you like a glass or orange or something?'

'Yes,' said Maura, 'It's close all right.'

(Oh, so *that* was why I used to see couples on the balcony . . . .)

'That was Carrie,' Maura said when we were sitting with our glasses of C & C. The blonde girl, one of her flatmates. She just had to talk to her about meeting up later: 'Sorry.' I waved that aside, more interested in what 'later' meant. Was Maura thinking what I was thinking, that there would be no parting us now, and later was a synonym for never? She and Carrie had been at Mercy together –

'You went to the Mercy?!' I was shouting again. You mean, I meant, that you were one of those girls we used to pass so snidely on our walks out Duckspool and Ballyneety, with the cerise uniforms and silly soup-plate hats – that you were on the far side of that cutting wall all that time? She and Carrie had probably been sizing me up for years (if they had any sense, they had)! She'd thought of me during night prayers, in domestic science. And here we were at last. Blessed smallness of the world! Wasn't life very simple after all? A mere matter of gales of giggling and lots of dancing. Oh Angel of God, my Guardian dear, keep nether man stowed safe below for me! Oh don't let me (him) spoil it. I vow and swear to you, Father Chaste Ukase of Veritas House, respect is all I have in my heart for her. (Pray for me.)

But she had to go, she really had to go; it was gone half-twelve. 'Ah don't.' I was far from ready for life to revert to cinders. But Carrie – oh that was it: the pal was an escape clause. (Yeah, I knew pals were great, I brooded nastily: Eddy is probably up against Miss Kelly in some doorway this very minute . . . .) And the lie of the land around the Four Provinces was so good, a shame to waste it; the porch of the old Harcourt Street station had to be designed with dancehall trysting in mind. And now she wanted to go to the cloakroom – well Jesus Christ! – leaving me feeling a right fool waiting for her. If the floor was thronged, the scene around the ladies' cloaks was a proper post-horn gallop. Gusts of powder, shrieks of laughter, hissed admonitions, lethal-sounding 'Excuse me's' filled the air. Flatfuls of disappointment stampeded out and towards the taxi-rank, handbags wheeling like Boadicean blades. Surprisingly cool-looking girls on their own emerged and, bums arcing in disdainful sway, went out to meet their swains (how come them lads knew enough to wait out on the street?).

At last! (Her smile immediately made me feel a fool no longer.)

'Listen,' I began, but synonyms for shift did not suggest themselves. Besides, Maura was a lot quicker. 'How about Sunday?' she said, reading my mind so well that she could let on, with a straight face, to be misreading it. She hurried out the address of the flat, the 'phone number (she had a 'phone!): 'About two?'

'No, but listen – '

Carrie had slipped by us to the street door, was pretending not to look.

'Goodnight, love,' said Maura simply, and reaching up, pecked me on the cheek.

I rocked. I rolled.

I had just received my first spontaneous kiss since First Communion Day, when the women who were in my life then, Mam and Chrissy, were momentarily overcome at the sight of puny me having reached the age of reason. It was only now, though, that I was really a hero. I'd got the girl.

3

The flat was in one of those solid, vaguely holy-looking houses in Sandymount Avenue, just beyond the railway gates on the left; an expensive, brownish, leathery, red-brick house in a much sedater part of the world than Leinster Road. I was afraid. Up until I'd got off the 18 and faced into that Sunday silence I felt fine. The various items that required attention had been attended to. My dinner of incinerated rashers, which I had more or less swallowed as soon as I got up, just in case the clock was slow or broke down somehow without my noticing (I didn't own a watch), was evidently not going to repeat on me. My tie was noose-straight. I'd aired the shirt I'd danced in by flapping it out the window for a few minutes – the act of a thorough-going tramp, I knew, but it was a rear window, so what harm? I may have even brushed my teeth, although it was the middle of the day.

The 18 dozed along. I had yet one more life-sustaining post-prandial cigarette and cleaned my nails with the spent match-stick – women were sticklers, you couldn't be too careful: and this was more important than a dance, this was broad daylight (this was my first date). I noticed that the sun was coming back for another of its little visits and I found myself nodding at the passing streets in a state of stupefied homage. World, world. Life, life. So good, so kind. Sweet Appian Way. Old RDS, by memory blessed. The cardboard (concrete?) nurse with the Sweep ticket held aloft, encouraging us all to chance our arm, was right, she was so right. I was approximately an hour and a half too early. By two, I was a wreck, and sweating smellily from walking to kill time.

And I was right to be afraid, I thought, when I saw the house up close. It was more ecclesiastical than at first sight. The door was flanked by stained-glass sidewindows depicting nothing except a pattern, which made me superstitious. The pattern did signify, yet remained a pattern, panes of blood and bile joined and disjoined by veins of lead, armorial bearing of the uncertain body, of which we are all scions, now and at the hour of our death – Get a grip on yourself, for the love of God! I stepped into the porch. The house engulfed me. I stood close to the door, as beggars tend to. The bell screeched. This is it. Throw the cigarette away – crisp footsteps on the cool tiled hall, mottled with pools of pale colour. Check the fly. This is it
. . . .

But what, exactly, was it? I would have been quite happy to sit and smoke and have a cup of tea and jaw and have another 143 cup of tea, as I might in the frontroom of my aunt or cousin I was visiting. But whether it was Maura saying, 'Won't be a tick, I'll just get my jacket', or one of the flatmates asking where were we going, in a tone that sounded barely on the polite side of ironical, it suddenly dawned on me that there was supposed to be a plan here. I was the man, wasn't I? What had I masterfully in mind? And tea out, no doubt, I thought uncomfortably, hearing the ghastly flap of empty pockets – and tomorrow's only Monday! I gave the flatmates an idiot grin, and shifted the weight on my feet. 'Oh, sit down!' they cried, which was not what I meant at all. I sat down. I offered around my cigarettes – clean me out altogether, why don't ye? But of course they didn't smoke. Instead their tense, wrinkle-resistant noses said, Filthy habit. They found a flowery saucer for my ash, which I by now was wishing I could deposit in my socks. It's the small things, I swear to God: they're the true crucifixional nails.

So we got the bus. That immediately made a big difference. The last time I was on a 7A or 8 going the Merrion Road, going in the wrong direction – well, at least that was behind me. We got into town. So far, so good. We got off at Suffolk Street. We walked around. Maura talked. I talked much more. She was a clerk/typist in a big insurance office. She earned seven quid a week. I winced. Retaliating, I wondered, patronizingly, if she liked the work, this *career*? It was a job, she said. I'd been told that girls were like this: tolerant, incurious, accepting. Mature. (How would I ever get anywhere with them?) 'Yes,' I said, impulsively, 'and it only cost five years of secondary school – of boarding-school – to get it.' There was a silence after that. I paused to admire my unexpected cynicism: it, I thought, made me sound older. I liked that. Must remember it. Thank you, Maura, I said silently, sincerely; you've already helped me see that there are images I've barely even glimpsed yet, never mind tried on. Helping me was the whole point, of course (amazing how quickly she'd got it – without seeming to think about it, really: oh, they were rare and fine indeed in their maturity, girls . . .).

We walked – what with that and my dancing, she must have thought I didn't like her legs. But I never noticed her legs. Now that I think of it, I don't believe she was a body for me at all. Just a presence: when I embraced her it was the 'my own' that

144

was the one I held. I remember that Sunday we sat in Stephen's Green for a while, and I put my arm around her shoulders. I noticed she, though still looking straight ahead at the ducks in the lake, seemed also a little more attentive, as though waiting. What for? I'd hardly thought I'd ever do more than dream of freedom I was now exercising, my arm mainly on the back of the bench, just respectfully resting across her shoulders, sun playing on the back of my hand, hair mildly tickling the back of my hand, sun turning the tendrils of her red hair to gold. This was it. The rest of the city was stretched out in couples all around us. I was happy, too. This was Chris plus feeling. Did Maura want more?

'Come on,' I said at length, realizing I had to make some kind of move. 'I'll show you the statue of Clarence Mangan. He was a right quare fella. Did ye do 'The Time of the Barmecides'? There was a lad a year ahead of me who used to call that 'The Time of the Bare Backsides'! But Mangan – he had something to do with Meath Street, I think. Were you ever up there around the Liberties? It's strange – different. I'll show you – '

Yes! – I could be Da and Maura me!

But, strange to say, she had a distant, somewhat tight-lipped look.

We went to the Crystal, we had a second honeymoon at the Four Provinces, we went to the Adelphi, the Carlton, the Regal and the Ritz, Ballsbridge, which had a great pong of Jeyes fluid, worth enduring only because I thought it of vital importance that Maura see *The Magnificent Seven*. She said she liked it. I think she pretty much liked everything we did, up to a point, but I can't be sure about this because I never gave her a chance to have her proper say. What can she have been thinking – what novenas she must have made to St Francis de Sales, patron of the deaf – as I told her that of course *The Magnificent Seven* was all Japanese, and that basically I knew everything about the cinema – 'they're not just pictures, you know' – because my father . . . . All I was trying to say was didn't she, like me, think it was great, that culture let us talk to each other. But I no more knew then that was what I meant, than I did with Chris. I didn't have to know it. Talk to me was its own justification, a freedom and delight synonymous with taking Maura   145 out. If girls were supposed to be pleasure machines, Maura was my microphone.

And it wasn't just for helping me break my silence that I treasured her. She was also turning me into a born-again Dubliner. Going by bus was an adventure again. Being downtown when the last house of the Metropole got out was the same old childish blare of bright lights and hoarse motors in the dark. And I had this little short-cut to show her and this little anecdote – 'Daddy used to take me to Alexandra Basin to see the big ships'; 'There's The Moira . . . ' – so that I began to see again that the city was as big as I'd originally thought. I saw myself as somebody with memories (would she never tire of giving me new images of myself?): therefore I was somebody – even if memories were only stains left by dried-up desires. But I might desire again, mightn't I? After all, I was only finding this out because I had been right about dancing, whose life of atmosphere and accident, music and mutuality, of the personal filtered through a public show to become at once more personal and less isolating, had proved itself by this person being beside me – this radiant window, this chance to pretend I could start all over again one more time.

What can I do? What can I do? I wanted us to be able to do something to show I was grateful and appreciative, something in the name of my memories and in the spirit of my desires. Dickie Rock and the Miami were all very fine and *King of Kings* profound. But they weren't new experiences. And I didn't want to turn us into tourists by suggesting, say, the National Gallery. To be mere sight-seers in one's own capital seemed awfully infra-dig; if there were sights they'd have to be my unexpected selections (besides, I knew nothing about paintings). Rainbow trout and chips at The Moira would have been ideal, but the memory of Franz flashing his wad reminded me that I was now, and always had been, paid in singles.

I don't know how it was I hit on the theatre. It may have been that *Philadelphia, Here I Come!* was the talk of the town; a strange phenomenon, a home-made hit, by someone who seemed – on the basis of our not knowing the first thing about him – not a bit like Brendan Behan. So, we went to see it at The Olympia, and that was strange too; the façade that seemed made of almond paste, the glass awning leading from street to box office, the atmosphere inside which was much more opulent and cathedralish than that of cinemas (which in comparison were merely parish churches). Yes, this was what I had in mind, something rich and strange – the naked stage an altar, the text's inviolable words, the whole production like the facts of life with its confidence tricks of tragicomic puppetry. And this play itself was gas; it was under our noses, not over our heads, not like that tongue-twisting, roller-coastering, larger-than-life Shakespeare (the world's only playwright, bar Behan). We all knew the hero Gar O'Donnell. We knew him so well that, at the end, we weren't laughing half as much as squirming, yet that was pleasure, too, kind of – or at least there was pleasure of a sort in not being entirely sure, in thinking . . . .

In any case, I'd found it (oh wasn't Dublin great for still hanging onto things for me to discover): the theatre, pictures for grown-ups, pictures sans machine – that's why it was Big Church . . . . I started taking Maura to the Abbey, at that time playing at the Queens in Pearse Street near the railway bridge, a step or two below the Olympia as to façade and appointments, though this was only to be expected in something so historical. Being part of our heritage it was as entitled to look dilapidated as any of the other parts. The Olympia, on the other hand, was only a theatre. The Abbey wasn't dependent on appearance: like all our, and my, most exigent and worshipful realities, it was an idea. It was exciting to ring reserving tickets, to dash in by bus during lunchtime to buy tickets, to push to the cowpat green glass doors to the foyer. It was as though such mundanities were really expressions of faith in and visible allegiance to this small vatican of art. Weren't their posters virtually the Pope's yellow (especially when wet with rain)? Wasn't the woman and hound only a more militant Virgin and Child?

There was a musty smell. A string trio (refugees from the Savoy) played thin but spirited music, a sound like that old ladies with a bit of go in them might make after a schooner of Christmas port. Bizet's l'Arlesienne Suite was top of the pops, with Grieg's Peer Gynt at number two; they never could get poor Anitra to dance right. Then the traditional knocks, the swish of curtain – and action! We saw a John B. Keane, a Louis D'Alton or two, and the three O'Caseys. There was Eileen Crowe looking down her nose at all around her, there was   147

Philip O'Flynn playing Fluther, flapping his arms as if indeed he had a feather to flutter; there was Harry Brogan sounding very like the resonant reciter who advertised cakes by Gate-aux on the wireless, Saturday afternoon at two. And standing behind them all was this O'Casey. I'd heard his name before. I explained to Maura: 'He had his name in the paper the time of the Tóstal.' 'What for?' she reasonably inquired, drawing out the Uncle Pether in me. Thwarted, I retorted, 'Something about a play, what else?' Still he seemed fascinating, in spite of notoriety – different from Behan, that way. His plays were a great laugh, spoiled sometimes, but not for long, by bombs and bullets. He was a slumster. He was a Protestant. I went to Rathmines Library and read up on him. He was a Communist. He lived in England. All this, I reported back to Maura, explained the Tóstal business. 'He must be a hell of a man,' I said, 'living with all them contradictions.'

Maura smiled wanly.

I came to at once. 'Cripes! – sorry!' I took her hand.

'What?' she seemed surprised.

'I said a curse,' I said: was that the right thing to call "hell"?'

'It's not that,' Maura said.

Well, that's good, I said to myself. I wouldn't for the world defile her presence with a dirty word. The only way to keep her was to maintain the respect mode, wasn't it?

'See you Friday?'

'Yes, okay.'

A quick hug in the porch, then off with me, whistling, hoping the last 18 hadn't gone, happy as a lark after another grand night out.

I had to talk to her even when I couldn't see her. Maura didn't like being called at work, and Mrs O'Connell reserved the 'phone in the house for her exclusive use. But there was a 'phone box at the bottom of Leinster Road, by the library, and thither I'd repair after my dinner of baked beans and white pudding, say, on the Mondays, Tuesdays and Thursdays that we agreed to wash our hair and have an early night, because we wanted to keep our jobs, didn't we? – naturally, I hadn't told Maura that I had more or less lost mine, in case she thought I couldn't afford the fabulous excursions into culture that were our love life.

There was always a line of people outside that 'phone box. We were penitents with downcast eyes. We were supplicants, waiting impatiently for our fortunes to be told. We were drunkards, craving to be slaked, jigging from foot to foot, scrounging cigarettes from each other. Inside it was sweaty and smoky. The receiver was hot and slippery. There were names and numbers all over the place, some in frail, hurried script, like the smoke from votice candles, more in confident strokes like the ads in the papers thanking St Anthony, St Jude, St Maria Goretti 'for favours received (publication promised)'. This atmosphere, these scribblings, suggested to me why others used the 'phone box ('put your sweet lips'). But I just called to see how Maura was getting on, to confirm the – to me – unforgettable arrangements for our next meeting for fear I forgot them; to be, as embarrassing hindsight makes all too clear, a bloody nuisance. I remember once standing for half an hour to call and ask her how to wash a shirt. 'I have to have it for Wednesday night.' I anxiously explained. 'Wear the one you're wearing,' Maura laughed, exasperated. But didn't she understand? – I was trying to do the right thing. Didn't she see? – I wanted to be with her all the time. Didn't she realize? – her job was to make me feel good about myself, so that I could ignore the things that hadn't gone, and weren't going, according to childish longing.

She should have taken all that in by now: I'd spent enough time regaling her with it. Not with what I considered her duty to be. She would know that automatically, I imagined, when she heard the tale of my recent woe. I assumed that anybody who was prepared to listen would be prepared to enter into my version of the story. And because Maura let me talk – being too good natured to stop me in the first instance, then latterly I daresay too bombarded by my angst and dreams of a happy Dublin for myself to know exactly what to do – I found I had a story once again and applied myself with renewed interest to all its ins and outs, the silences, the inscrutable motives, the strange searing that lingers from hurt feelings and inhibits being touched. The more I went into it, the more lost Maura became, the more necessary she seemed, the more inclined I became to think that she could anchor me, like aunts of yore. I was doing the one thing that, I had heard, was absolutely fatal with wimmin, I was trying to be serious.

149

Maura broke it off. We were on her porch after another fascinating foray into theatreland, fresh from cutting capers on the floor of the Four P's, something madly sophisticated and disembodied anyhow, I'm sure. No, no; Maura was not being critical of the evening, or of any of the evenings, really; and indeed it was difficult not to agree that Harry Brogan was 'a darlin' man' (and laugh); undoubtedly, as I'd averred, the country was still maggoty with the likes of Donal Davoren, 'poet and poltroon', neither of us knowing the name of a living Irish, or any other, poet. Still, there I was, the perplexed milquetoast in the Thurber cartoon, trying to find words for what the caption put so well: 'With you Lydia, I have known happiness, and now you say you're going crazy.' Or so I see it when old enough to find anticlimax funny.

At the time, all I saw was a foundry of nails being slammed into a forest of coffins. She had pushed me out on an ocean of wormwood and gall without a paddle. I fucked culture for being unnatural (it was nothing but the city's piss-proud erection). I double-fucked respect. I should have remembered what we'd taught ourselves at school – the Four F's: find 'em, feel 'em, fuck 'em and forget 'em. I should have made her bed and got her to lie in it and not be turning myself into the horn of a dilemma. But I wasn't like that! Oh, what *mí-ádh* was on me at all that I couldn't see what the fuck was in front of me, that one talent which is death to hide . . . . Too fucking true. They also serve who only stand and wait – well, shit on that.

I swore I wouldn't 'phone, but of course I had to. Maura was out, though (a big lie: where did she have to go?): this was Carrie. 'She's after meeting a medical student, I think.' Aha, I might have known class would raise its ugly head. Of course, I wasn't good enough for her (Tallow – worse, Tallowish – turns down Lismore – of all the cheek!). So she was just like the rest of them, after all; chasing the oul' college scarf, girls' equivalent of a bit of skirt. But what I found myself saying was, 'She ought to introduce me; maybe he could have a look at my leg.'

'Why? What's up with it?' I could hear Carrie's ears begin to stiffen with the hint of news.

Where my story came from I have no idea, but what emerged was that I had spilled acid on my leg at work and that now it was a kind of festering greenish colour, and sore, not that it mattered a whole lot (stoically) – the implication being that I was going to hang up my dancing shoes in any case (wherever that load of cock-and-bull came from it clearly dates from before my discovery that real life can give rise to symbols!). Good Carrie condoled. The conversation limped on a minute or two more; then we had to go.

'I suppose ye're going to the Ags tomorrow night?' I swear – I didn't know that was what I'd called about!

The Capitol were playing, it'd be dear, but there was nothing else for it. And there they were, Maura looking as sweet and dapper as if she didn't have a care in the world. Hello! Surprise! Look, not even limping! I saw her jaw faint, and *oh shit!* was written all over her face. 'I thought,' she began, grimly; 'your leg – '

'Aw c'mon,' I interrupted, plaintively, hand out.

But no. Suddenly there was nothing else for what, exactly?

I watched from the balcony for a while. I saw her stand and smooth her skirt down, give her hand and take to the anonymous, teeming floor, I realized that I'd been strangely mistaken: Maura was not me and I was not my father.

4

'God, no,' said the white girl, taking exception to the first thing out of my mouth. 'I *never* come here;' then, suspiciously, 'Do you?'

'Very seldom,' I lied suavely.

It was a pleasure to lie about the Sivilkems. The Sivilkems was a dead loss, a wash-out: enticing only to disappoint, pretending it could supplant anticlimax, only to reproduce it. And I hated it all the more because I seemed tied to it. That is, the belief persisted that I had to go out somewhere, and the Four P's Friday night was my lazy non-choice. Going further would only reward my forlorn hope of faring better with a longer walk home. Anyhow, anything, even a lie, to keep the conversation going. That was the main point, I now realized, 151 keep the ballroom ball rolling, play the game. That was the mistake I'd made with Maura: I'd acted like we were supposed to be more than dancing partners. Well, I wasn't going to make that mistake again. From now on I was going to go whichever way the wind blew. If the white girl had told me that she was the niece of Archbishop John Charles McQuaid and that after this, her first dance, her uncle was going to have the hall burned to the ground and everyone in it sent straight to hell, I probably would have replied, 'The blessings of God on the pair of ye.'

She said nothing, however, and we went on for a while with her putting me through her paces. I was a bad dancer, but she beat the band. And what was more, she didn't seem to care. There was I trying to disguise my expertise in the Bunion Boogie while she, quite detached (though in fact – *ouch!* – not detached enough), swung around in a vaguely satirical hobble, by which turkeyoid gait she expressed assent to the mechanics of foxtrot. I caught her meaning right enough; she was doing the henhouse when the fox is nigh. It was just that my brains didn't reach my feet. This was the Funky Chicken ahead of its time (I was the one laying the egg).

Nothing would do me, of course, but to find out if her idea was to show me personally up, to shame me before a putative rude and scoffing multitude (of what were wimmin not capable?), so I asked her out again for the slowing of the tempo right down, now ladies and gentlemen boys, etc. This time she did an exaggerated but technically proficient waltz (at least by my rickety standards), holding me sternly at arms' length and looking me up and down with a quizzical frown – milady nonplussed by the appearance of an uncalled-for servant. Clearly some kind of lunatic . . . . Just my luck . . . . Yet, after the slow set, when she announced abruptly that she was going home, I found myself saying, 'Hang on; I'll come with you.' A lunatic was better than nothing – much!

'It's okay,' she said; 'I live in Harrington Street,' as if the point was whether her place was just a hundred yards away or not. But as she spoke she stared stonily at me, so that I saw she wasn't being stupid, therefore neither should I be. Except now I was blowing in the wind. This new approach of mine, whereby I was not to reason why and thereby be in full command of the nothing I was doing was just as confusing as my earlier flying blind. It had somehow failed to occur to me that whenever I perpetrated passivity, proceedings would grind to a halt just as they'd always done. So I said, 'Can I see you again?' I could if I wanted, came the sceptical reply, and she strode through the rim of lads around the back of the hall, firming the day with arrangements thrown over her shoulder. A bit of a character, wasn't she? (Was I supposed to laugh, or what?) I would if she liked. But of course now that I was, if only on the strength of my perplexity and low-grade desperation, willing to play, *she* was deadly serious.

I called her the white girl because of her flour-and-margarine complexion, acquired because she ate nothing (she was saving up) and slept less. But I might just as well have called her the black girl. She wore black tops I'd never seen the like of, they being neither shirts nor blouses but half-baked chemises or singlets with sleeves. She wore them tucked in tight to her black or navy-blue skirt. Her black hair came unfashionably lanky down her shoulders. I'd never seen a woman dress so indifferently, so strikingly, so obviously in a way that neither nun nor man commended. She often went without stockings. Her legs were strong – bold, naked, white. Legs that spoke volumes. Outspoken, strident legs. What have I here at all? I wondered – some sort of new breed of Teddy Girl? She was nobody's machine, I could see that. She never wore make-up. She lived on coffee. She was saving to go to Paris.

That flouting walk of hers, which made her body seem to utter; her sense of image which seemed to denounce image; the way she knew her mind and spoke it: she was Dublin, I was convinced. Yet in some ways she was more ordinary than I was. She worked at the tax office in O'Connell Street, a job which smacked of pull to me, or brains, or luck, or whatever it was I lacked, the very sort of niche that parents prayed for, and with good pay, too, and benefits. She was from Cavan. I said I'd never been there; was it like Carrickmacross at all? 'Much too much,' said Mary sourly. But she had a large family of brothers there and liked to hitchhike back at weekends. I wondered if it wasn't dangerous, cadging lifts, a girl alone? Mary sneered as though I'd belittled her: 'Only for the drivers,' she growled, adding if there was one thing she really hated it was stupid statements.

153

She talked a lot about what she hated. I wasn't used to hearing someone being *against* things. (Had I been wrong all this time in wanting to be for?) She spoke with power. I was enthralled. Her performance on the Sivilkems floor, which I had labelled foolery or worse, had been the height of serious-ness, I now learned: she hated dancehalls. 'It's nothing but a big cattle market,' she complained; 'fellas spitting on their hands at the thought of you – don't they even call us heifers. That's why I dance like an *óinseach*. It makes them mad, and they leave me alone, which is where I'd rather be in the first place, if gropers like them are the best I can do.' And this reminded her. 'Don't you be getting any ideas either,' she went on severely; 'none of that stuff; no involvement; I'm not interested, okay?' Grand, grand, I agreed; cards on the table, much better that way, mine not to reason why . . . . And I noted, with a vague sense of relief, that she found it difficult to talk about; it really was a hateful subject.

And Mary hated the job as well, pushing papers, answer-ing 'phones, making tea, doing a bit of shopping for the boss at lunchtime (while he went to the Parnell Street Mooney's); and there were little hutches to which people could come in off the street and be rude to you. Besides which, tax was boring, tax was stupid, the whole country was tax-mad – punitive Church and weary family, hopeless government and boarding-schools: each took its toll. It was hard to believe she'd given two years of her life to it. Except, of course, what choice was there in this balls of a country? Well, anyhow, she'd soon be well out of it. Paris for Christmas. Ring out the bells!

The no-ness of her overawed me. How wonderfully black and white she was. How splendidly unconfused. (Saying no: what a simple way to avoid confusion!) What wouldn't I give to be as definite as her, to quit as being unworthy of me a probably pensionable clerkship. 'Do you speak French?' Mary just laughed, and her long hair swung like an arc of water. '*Non!*' She didn't care. I thought of people from my previous life for whom there also had to be a France, a different place to learn from, where perhaps (was that why Da went?) the present might be full enough to allay the rest. And now there goes that brazen Mary. She's made of herself a flag to follow. I looked up to her, cringing with jealousy and hunger.

154

And a little fear. She was too tough, I thought. She forced herself. (She should have been more like me . . . .) She didn't sleep. The room in Harrington Street had no light. She was turning her stomach into a coffee-grounds mine. It was the dark room I found preying on me, probably because I never saw it, never would see it, could only try to picture it. (It looked chilling and fascinating, like Mary herself. I suppose I also saw in it an image of my own vague feelings of lostness and hapless groping, feelings made a little more insistent by dancehalls' unrewarding gloom and the heavy, unaccommodating shadows of Maura's porch.) The darkness didn't bother Mary one bit, however. It saved money. 'I won't be living there long,' she said, 'and I'm never there now.'

If she wanted to read she went to the reading-room at Kevin Street library. With all the smells and snoring? That unnerved me too. 'Well, what about them?' Mary demanded contentiously. Those shelterers with nothing only time to call their own were, she'd have me know, a lot better company than others she could name: they did less harm, they never made to paw her, they didn't pretend to be anything they weren't, their lapel pockets weren't lined with fountain pens and propelling pencils. 'Read George Orwell,' she commanded.

'Ah, *Animal Farm*,' I said, assuming this to be a relevant title, though really I was fleeing for cover: I wasn't used to someone taking me on, to someone who had an active, challenging code of face values.

'No, no,' she went impatiently, and loaned me *Down and Out in Paris and London*, though this only caused another little flare-up and for me more intellectual discomfort. I liked the story fine. The only thing, I complained, was that I couldn't tell if it was true or false, fiction or real life story. 'What does it matter?' Mary demanded disdainfully. 'Everything is true in its own way.' I blanched at this novel gospel. I'd always thought everything was true in a pre-ordained way, a way which was controlled by something that was both in, and alien to, its nature: father and son, work and worker, God and man . . . . What kind of person was this Cavanite at all, who made me feel so woefully conventional? I had to know: it was as though I hoped her fearlessness, her restlessness, would prove contagious and would sponsor me, somehow, in hard manhood and loveless venturing. And for all my backward- 155 ness, she let me stay in tow.

I was so grateful for her grand bad company I even joined her in sleeplessness, otherwise known as the Studio Club, one or two small dank rooms upstairs in Dawson Lane, where you could go at any time, it seemed, as long as it was way late, to see strange people and drink watery Maxwell House or sometimes cider. Strange women roared with laughter here and went in holey stockings, flat-heeled shoes. Strange men gave out choruses of songs that seemed familiar in principle but were, once I paid attention, totally unknown to me. Strange Mary stood in the midst of all, an impious candle in her black garb and bright white face, at home at last and animated in her proud difference.

Of course I had seen people like this before. These were members of the maimed fraternity who played in public places, appealed to the charity of cinema queues, stared vaguely heavenward with eyes like flawed glass marbles, singing uncontrollably some *passé* song. I was, it seemed, in the company of such fixtures' sons, the pre-maimed, whose turn at immobility would surely come and who were assembling now to pass on parental tips and train each other for the rocky road. Tramps. How knowledgeable Mrs O'Connell was after all; how clearly she'd discerned the lie of the land, the shape of things to come. Had she felt in the air the ousting of her repertoire, her dreadful crooning acting like some crone-like antennae?

Some of the lads seemed to be disabled already, with mouth-organs strapped prosthetically to their guitars. But they were happy. Their clothing might be as dun as dirt, but as long as they could twiddle out the notes, ignore the barber and act like life was a prolonged fair day, what care they? I couldn't make head or tail of them. They could be a resurrection of the Unemployed. They could be what happened to a Film Society that had been forced to hock all its machinery. Once again, though there was no balcony, I took to doing what I had always done so well. I watched from a distance, wondering.

But were these people proper folk-singers? I daren't ask Mary, needless to say; my ignorance continually offended her, and the nicest thing she could think of to do was introduce me
to men up to their eyes in turf-mould (mere beard is under-

statement), to whom I couldn't possibly open my mouth, having too much to say. It was disturbing, though, never to hear 'Master McGrath' (the national anthem of West Waterford). And how about 'Kevin Barry'? It confused me greatly that the songs being sung were clearly Irish yet were most obscure. And in any case, hadn't Irish stuff had its day? We were in the age of Pelvic Man and 'Jailhouse Rock' now. Irish had served its purpose – fair dues to it: *de moturis nil nisi bonum* (unless you wanted seven years' bad luck). We were well shut of the English, which nobody would deny. And lest we forget, the language was compulsory at school: if you failed it you failed everything. But everybody knew that the life underwritten by the language belonged to the time of the bare backsides. Didn't we wear the *crios* and Aran ganzy, paupers' chic, to prove we were a different breed, complete now with rural electrification? Yet, folk was modern too. The Clancy Brothers were the latest thing. The broadsides they belted out spoke of an unfamiliar nation, a loose young nation not afraid to stamp its feet on the holy ground and roar, 'Fine girl y'are', the girl who had (did they mean? was it possible?) sanctified the sod by stretching herself out on it in lively and obliging fashion – the very opposite in type and temperament to tubercular Noreen Bawn, lying stretched cold ('There's a graveyard in Tirconnell'), whose obsequies were conducted in slow waltz time.

What if the music at the Studio Club owed nothing to electricity – thought impressionable me – it rattled away with spunk and verve all the same. Nobody danced to it: but I was getting tired of dancing anyhow. I'd try singing, which made the brain dance. I listened, drinking down copious quantities of intoxicating *fol-de-dol-day* with *toorle-aye* chasers. The message to Jim Reeves seemed plain: he'd have to go.

We went to a hall somewhere around Capel Street behind the Four Courts. There were forms scattered around and thin young men and thin older men and freckled young women who wore their buttoned-up overcoats all evening long sat on them. Every so often, after a few desultory words together, one of the men would get up and take a flute or tin-whistle from inside his jacket and bend his face to it to moan a slow air or trill a jig. Sometimes fiddlers and melodeonists turned up. 157

They were nondescript too, clean-shaven and quiet-spoken. Decent skins. Respectable young men. Anonymous. They too sank themselves into their playing, submerging self so the tunes might have life, eyes closed, sharing their secret lives with small audiences in a cold hall. Nothing else in life, their playing said, evinces or encourages this rapture.

During the day, perhaps, they served at Dockrells, they were links in the Civil Service paper chain, they unobtrusively supervised the Mauras and the Marys, were subject merely to the customary quotas of paranoia, misanthrophy, dyspepsia, despair. They had a pint and a half-one before the Kimmage bus; made the First Fridays. But secret lives would out, evenings once a month or so in the city gave way to hauntings of stone and heather and empty strands, dancing firelight and the curlew's cry. It was good the youngsters were coming along. Maybe some of them would team up together (*together*, that's the ticket), keep out of the mouse race, stay away from the sullenness of women bored at home. The times they were a-changing – please God. They might manage to fall in with Ó Riada.

There wasn't any singing at Capel Street, or perhaps it was drowned out, because as soon as we began going there, it seemed, the whole town was at it, and anyone who had a loft or a back room had a folk club. After closing time on Friday nights, Ronnie Drew and his merry men held forth like heroes at the Grafton News and Cartoon Cinema, songs from O'Casey (I thought, not to mention Prussia Street) and the common tongue. How the audience roared and rollicked, singlets saturated with sweated booze, primed expectantly by the occasion's evanescent anarchism. Mary always hoped Luke Kelly would be there. He often was. She loved Luke Kelly. The raw passion of his voice could start a free-for-all or stop a train. Everyone loved Luke Kelly.

It was at the Grafton, too, that I first heard the singing of Joe Heaney. That oboe: that voice of quartz. And for the first time I tried to take in the *via dolorosa* paced out by his repertoire. He didn't supply *folderols*, which made it hard: there was no joining in. He sang in our native language (the one not taught at school, the one he lived through). That made it hard, too: he was a stranger. And I knew some of the words, because we'd done 'Caoineadh na dTrí Muire' and 'Anach Cuain' for the

Leaving. Why that made listening to Joe Heaney hard was that I never knew these works were songs. I only knew them as tortuous demonstrations of syntax and vocabulary which had to be mastered 'for the exam', an exercise which was the intellectual equivalent of Uncle Seamus sitting on his arse swatting green-fly. Only now did I learn that these poem-songs were part of a man's life, and that he thought them worth denoting to life at large (the audience). Every time he performed them, a notion of the people filled the air, permitting harmony. At the end of every song Joe Heaney sang there was a small moment of silence while we reckoned, flinching slightly (I felt vaguely cheated), with the nerve he touched, the something missing in us that had been laid bare (language and silence attaining synonymity), while we returned from the uplifting, windswept territory of the artist and his work.

So, this is why, I thought, Mary is a folkster. She loves the people. The city doesn't offer what she knows – or rather feels – of age and rootedness. She can't take the hurry and the flesh (it's only late, when that's all over, that she comes into her own). She knows she hates the not-them – the Medical Students, the Institutes' Associate Members. If Paris, mother of liberty, is the name she gives to all she loves, that's certainly as good a name as anyone can invent. But it's on the stage I'll find her one of these fine times, the Juliette Greco of Usher's Island, war to the death against nine-to-fivery and all its works and pomps in the green glint of her eyes, in her every posture.

I was dead wrong, of course. One evening she just didn't turn up. I slunk unconfidently to the Studio Club. No sign. I hung around outside her place in Harrington Street a time or two. It was uncomfortable looking up at the windows from the steps of the CYMS opposite: the windows were opaque, like sea under cloudy sky, like the pupils of the blind. The evenings were drawing in. It was getting cold. (Besides, I didn't know her window.) At last I went one lunchtime to the tax office. A clerk my own age, her age, in be-dandruffed blazer and Pioneer pin, huffily gave me the official word. 'Mary's gone.' Now here I was with something much simpler and more provocative than my image of her – her power of decision.

5

It seemed a fine idea, though, the people, so I spent that October going after them. I pursued them to The Long Hall and The Palace Bar. I saw them in various Mooneys, in Rice's on the Green, in Lloyd's, North Earl Street. My pubbing was a Mary-substitute, no doubt, at least to begin with. She had introduced me to a new style of going out, and going drinking, apart from its humanistic dimension, seemed an agreeable modification of that style, a combination of doing the town and being an insider, of joining the general public and minding one's own business, a kind of date with oneself.

It wasn't long, however, before I learned that drink provided its own rationale. Mary was quite unnecessary. Everywhere I went there were strangers eager to teach me all about it. The grail of a good pint was much discussed and a civil house – 'Quiet, y'know; you can get on with the serious business of drinking in it' – was considered a boon surely. Grey-faced men in suits gave me elaborate specifications and explicit directions. There was a pub in Chatham Street that served a decent pint, ditto an establishment in Granby Row. And I suppose I tried them, avoiding betimes the purveyors of cat's piss and similar emollients whose name was evidently legion in the town and who sucked up to tourists – 'For the love o' God, son, steer clear of that shower.' Let nothing but familiarity ring, seemed to be the old soaks' watchword. As for myself, to drink became an opportunity merely to hide in plain sight.

'The usual, Mr O?' The barman rarely has to lift his eyes from the Limerick Junction returns. I am an old reliable, and he has the tipple served before I settle to the bar. My hand shakes, greeting my old, old friend. Its cool kiss enters me, tang of mud, tang of salt, tang of cleansing; my bitter-sweet preservative. But it would take years to get to that stage. (I know it's sacrilegious to speak of time and pubs together, but I knew no better, being young and hurried, a temporary state, mercifully.) Even more so than I had found before, drink was all slowness and minute gradations. The drawing of the pint. The pint's sluggish surge to form a head. The pint must sit. The head is capped. The glass must have its bottom wiped. The glass has to be slowly elevated, and the 'ah' slowly exhaled. And grey-faced men in greasy suits of navy-blue would tell me about cellarage and temperature, lingering on obscure points of environmental nicety in the manner of a loving father who only wants his favourite child to spoil him (it'd be only fair). All too often, however, numb from the application of minutiae, I would omit to pay my interlocutor his fee. When he at length formally brought his dissertation to a close by raising his glass with a flourish and lowering in one draught his remaining third of beer, all I could think to do was watch the fluttering Adam's apple and listen to the glottal gulping (ever the spectator). This caused the other – so friendly so recently – to move off, muttering, and made me conclude that people were strange.

If there were pubs where young people went, they went to them together, and without me. I never saw anyone my own age drinking on his own. And of course there never ever were solo drinking girls – the very idea! If there were pubs with people on their own in them, the people looked old no matter what their age, and down at heel, looked as though life had forgotten them and that they weren't too surprised it had. But I could have seen these people anywhere, there were broken men wherever I'd been; my past was peopled with victims of narcoleptic consciences, stunned consciousnesses (the population of Lismore). I couldn't think of anything to say to them, and usually they took no notice of me, since I was just as nondescript as themselves – more noticeably so, if anything, not being a regular. Only if you were real hard up would you think of bumming a pint off me. I added to the counter's age the ringed imprint of my glass and went on my way.

And never a hint of folk. I wasn't looking for songs and singers: they were easy to find. What I was after was a bit of the Grafton buzz, the flavour of carousel and relaxation. Weren't pubs places where such moods were rehearsed, their air loud with O'Caseyish remonstration, Behanish bonhomie; where the Prussia Street pantomime found permanent form and the binman's circus was forever on parade. But all pubs gave unginger me the scrape of chairs and the stench of gents. Was it that folk and people were not the same at all? – another dirty trick of culture.

I sat upstairs in Doran's, Marlborough Street, with its lounges along the walls and good class ashtrays and string of 161 fairy lights fringing the shelf above the till. I was looking at my future in a pint of Spatenbrau, but could see nothing. (Well, maybe in the next one.) For the time being, I told myself that I liked this beer's blondeness. I liked its foreignness. And I hadn't yet met anyone wanting to tell me all about it. Early evening. There was a couple in a corner, he in a crumpled suit, her hair *en bouffant*. I heard low laughter, glasses clinking. I heard new banknotes speak like a fortune-teller's cards being turned, like crisp tongues of flame. All around were appoint-ments in plastic and off-red. I felt depressed.

But I had high hopes of Jo Locke's. These were based not so much on the proprietor's musical accomplishments. Frequent regurgitations of his 'Goodbye' from *The White Horse Inn* on Radio Éireann's Hospitals Requests had made me think that he was to vocalizing what Jack Doyle was to the noble art of self-defence. But Ruritanian connotations were nowhere to be found here: the pub was plainly named 'Jo Locke's Singing Pub'. Well now, thought I, here's something being put on by someone who's seen the world a bit. This should be good. And I made straight for that upstairs on Aston Quay. There was a microphone and a piano. You gave your name to an M.C., who was also the pianist, and sat until your number came up, drinking. Drink came via waiter, so all there was to do was wait. Talk was dangerous. People were loudly shushed for trying to spoil the granny's birthday or Johnny's return with Luton Vauxhall money. The Johnnys mainly put their sweet lips, or sometimes remembered the Red River valley, very slow and low. All concerned had as politely passive a time as possible. Did I sing? I was, rather, to be found heading as quickly in the opposite direction as three pints on an empty stomach would permit.

The opposite direction was the one taken by the empty mid-evening bus, and more memorable than my attempt to blend beer and the milk of human kindness is what happened in the aftermath of the abortive blur. Still teetering a little, I got off the bus and made for the Leinster Chalet, or rather chalet-not, since the place bore no resemblance to matters Swiss or skiful, except perhaps in the sense of being a last resort – it stayed open till midnight. There, however, I could make plans to satisfy the fierce hunger created by the drink. I'd buy two
162   eggs, three sausages, three rashers, a turd of black pudding,

which raw material I would clutch to my shirt, appetitiously and greasily, while at the same time (no easy feat) negotiating the Leinster Road and the rapidity with which railings, gateways, steps and keyholes thrust themselves at the tipsy, egg-bearing traveller.

Everything went in the pan at once and was immediately set fire to. Giant eructations of smoke filled the room (a tricky business, bending over boozed to adjust the gas jet). Steam from the saucepan befogged the drapeless window – quick! rinse out the mug under the cold tap, wipe sodden hands down leg of trousers, shovel dust of Maxwell House in. A smell of singeing rose where fag had slipped from rim of old spaghetti-tin ashtray onto the tablecloth of *Sunday Times*. But lovely grub – muck in! muck in!

But this orgy of bedsitterland *gemütlichheit* had its toll, once I toppled into bed. I was all for repose, being sated, but the bed rejected me, and turned into a disorienting engine. Round and round it spun me, petrified and paralysed (perhaps it was too many years of suchlike dislocation which had my greasy-suited pubmen the way they were). It was like my childhood nightmares when the terroristic imagination cut off legs and had me frighteningly wrong way round in bed, unable to straighten up and fly right. Or was I being punished for culinary overconfidence, as my addresses in spate to the sink suggested? Weakened and quivering, I'd clutch the side of the polluted trough like the thin figures in the middle distance at Dolphin's Barn long ago after their canal swim. Except that they had immersed themselves, whereas I had been evacuated. Was Dublin now merely an emetic, reducing me to merely being a body? I felt empty.

The clock ticked. It was November. Leaves slapped soggily against the window. Wind did its doleful number in the wires. Snatches of 'Friday Night Is Music Night' came from the Home Service of the retired *chanteuse* in the room next door. Doors banged downstairs, doors of cars outside, cars raced away to pleasure. I wasn't going out: I knew there was nothing to go out to. Only one bar of the electric fire worked. Seven-thirty. Eight. I went to bed.

To get warm, of course. But I let on I went to bed to read. I would have preferred a radio. But I couldn't have one and buy 163 books as well, and I had to buy books, otherwise life would have been just a tissue of necessities, a holding operation for the body only. I wanted to tell myself that things hadn't come to that yet.

Perhaps because I didn't have a radio, I went through a bout of reading American books. They had great titles – *For Whom the Bell Tolls*, *The Sound and the Fury* . . . . But Faulkner was unlike any America I'd ever seen, and besides was tumultuous and broody. As for the Hemingway, it obscenitied in the milk of my impatience and I couldn't be bothered to finish it (the Stella was bound to have the movie of it, anyhow, some Sunday night). I wanted every book to be George choking the Lenny in me, to be Rose of Sharon unbuttoning to nurse me. Yet when I tried other Steinbecks, they seemed somehow both ponderous and thin. James Dean was better than *East of Eden*.

No book would have satisfied me. Once upon a time (eighteen months previously, that is), I had taken to books as I might have to kept promises. They had involved me in desires. They'd shown ideas, images. Those days were gone. My mind was a leaden cloud. Nothing could hold it. Nothing held me now. Outsiders might be interesting to read about, I told myself, but in reality they're nothings. If there's nothing outside there's only an emptiness within. And there was nothing new in Dublin. I went to see *Billy Liar*. It was only funny. They should have made it true (but they never did in pictures, did they?). So I still didn't know what I was going to do after Christmas, when Ken let me go. All thought kept turning to the past. Failed boyfriend, failed drunkard. And behind those two loomed earlier ones, Monkstown, Harcourt Street, which I'd considered deliverances at the time, but could only see now as larger, more decisive failures. Book propped unattended against raised knees covered by ratty quilt, I stared off into the space that was my nothingness. I was going to have to make my mind up. I was going to have to act as though there was a mind to be made up (there had to be more than feelings to be hurt in there). I was going to have to be a Mary, and decide. I never had done that before. I never thought that I would have to pass this Leaving.

I was reduced to a bone, the bone that pointed arrogantly at nothing, the miniature 'I' that dominated a father who only wanted to reject it, who beat it till it cried.

The machine that revved and revved and overheated and coughed up oil.

That body which, quivering, caused more distress and shame than even Guinness-puke.

The surge of novelty, that banal repetition. Loving Dublin, the oul' rag and bone shop itself.

'Fog is a good sign,' said Peg, brightly. 'Looks like you'll have a smooth crossing, anyway.'

The North Wall, 4 January, 1965. I'd been thirty months in Dublin, and this was the anticlimactic climax: I was leaving.

We stood on the ferry deck, waiting for Da to arrive. We had come early, I'd already stowed the bag in the cabin. All around us exciting clanks and bangs rang out in the viscous, diesel-laden air. Latecomers hurried aboard out of the raw evening, dragging Dunne's Stores bags full of the husks of Xmas back to their lives 'over', their real lives. Behind Peg, the city was a rumour in the mist, a remote settlement in some non-milky way. 'Still no sign of him,' Peg said every so often. 'No,' I replied. There seemed nothing else to say.

It was Peg who told me to book a berth, and who had rung Da to tell him I was going. That was about as much talk as my decision caused. When I announced it, I assumed my audience (Peg and Mam, up from Lismore for Christmas) would be taken aback by the boldness of the move, a leap into the unknown worthy of a moral Tarzan. They would protest, I thought (hoped). I would insist. I'd inform them that they'd had their chance. I'd say with gleeful callousness that they should stop their gobs by inserting money in them: 'How about this?' I planned to say, swaggering a little, having them for once where I wanted them; 'send me for a year to do First Arts.' There would be tears. Their patent crocodility I'd repudiate with stony silence. I'd press my point. No faller for Christmas spirit I: they needn't try that. Goodwill, my hole! The only good was -bye. (I just hoped Mam would not start litanizing my mistakes to me. Just let not that happen.) But opportunities arose for neither.

To my great surprise, I found that my announcement caused no great surprise. I would be as well off, if not better, I was told. It was as though I had only just found out what they had known for years: Ireland was a banjaxed country and Dublin a slough of despond. The difference between us was that I was not prepared to offer up being Irish for the Holy Souls or otherwise accept it as an expression of God's recognizable yet inscrutable sense of humour (all kings had clowns: thus the King of Kings had a countryful of favourite dwarfs and suchlike, blessed imps of innocence and back-chat). If to live was, willy-nilly, what I'd chosen to do (God help me), then I'd have to go. Besides, O'Briens who had crossed before me had all done well. There was the example of Uncle Frank, the engineer, to spur me on. He'd gone to England but hadn't stopped, went on to Africa, to Canada, saw awesome Holy Week in Seville while stationed with the Air Ministry in Gibraltar, was at that very moment off to Australia (keep the sunny side up).

Still, Mam was sad at parting. She gave me a fiver. I gave her a perfunctory hug, impatient, accepting that impatience as confirmation of the stranger I had become. And I knew enough (had seen enough movies) to realize that strangers kept on moving. Even in Ireland, looking back on it (and I liked looking back), I hadn't been able to stop. School, Lismore, Enniscorthy, Dublin. Up and down and over and back. Welcome everywhere, belonging nowhere: the welcome a preamble to just another leaving: the human *Rawhide* theme, that's me.

Come on, come on. Let's go, let's go. I felt bound for Treasure Ireland. I kept politely suggesting to Peg that there was no need for her to stay, she'd only get pneumonia standing out here. 'Ah no, no,' she protested. Had my going to be seen to be believed? No: it was just Peg being dutiful again, being beside the point practically speaking, being ritualistically crucial. I wished she'd stop muttering about Da's delay, though. It uncharitably occurred to me that she was staying to see if he did turn up. He did. The three of us stood around in silence, pressing cigarettes on each other.

The hooter sounded, saving us from ourselves. We shook hands. Between Da's hand and mine, a note.

'Sorry it can't be more,' he said.

Sorry!

'That's all right,' I said.

All right!

166   I went below and lay on the bunk. The *Hispaniola* pulled

away. I shared the cabin with a stocky Scotsman who fetched tea for us and laced it with Johnny Walker. I slept a dreamless sleep. At Birkenhead I woke in panic to nightmarish pounding. But it was nothing to do with me: they were letting off the cattle. Then we drifted, a strange motion between movement proper and genuine purpose. But it had nothing to do with me.

There was the Royal Liver building with the cock on top. That was on the cover of the insurance book we had in Lismore. Then Lime Street (Mallow) and the London (Dublin) train. Cows ran away from us. Crewe was Limerick Junction with a swelled head. Dank green, in forty shades, flashed by. We cantered through Nuneaton, or was that Portlaoise? The air at Euston was smashing, everything I wanted it to be – frying, coffee and exhaust fumes. And look at all those beautiful red buses . . . .